Gods and Arms

Gods and Arms

On Religion and Armed Conflict

Edited by
Kjell-Åke Nordquist

The Lutterworth Press

The Lutterworth Press
P.O. Box 60
Cambridge
CB1 2NT
United Kingdom

www.lutterworth.com
publishing@lutterworth.com

ISBN: 978 0 7188 9316 3

British Library Cataloguing in Publication Data
A record is available from the British Library

First published by The Lutterworth Press, 2013

Copyright © Trossamfundet Svenska Kyrkan
(Church of Sweden), 2013

Published by arrangement
with Pickwick Publications

Contents

Contributors

R. Scott Appleby— Professor of History and John M. Regan Jr. Director, Kroc Institute for International Peace Studies, University of Notre Dame, Indiana, USA

Göran Gunner—Researcher at Church of Sweden Research Unit, Associate Professor in Christianity and Interreligious Studies, Uppsala University, Uppsala, Sweden

Mariyahl Hoole—Research Associate, National Peace Council, Colombo, Sri Lanka

Mark Juergensmeyer—Professor of Sociology and Director of The Orfalea Center for Global & International Studies, University of California, Santa Barbara, California, USA

Anne N. Kubai—Associate Professor and Researcher at the Hugo Valentin Centre, Uppsala University, Uppsala, Sweden

Kjell-Åke Nordquist—Visiting Professor, Stockholm School of Theology, Stockholm, Sweden and Associate Professor, Department of Peace and Conflict Research, Uppsala University, Uppsala, Sweden

Jehan Perera—Doctor of Law, Executive Director, National Peace Council, Colombo, Sri Lanka

Jennifer Schirmer—PhD, Research Professor and Projects Director, Conflict Analysis & Peace Dialogues, University of Oslo, Oslo, Norway

Nari Senanayake—Research Associate, National Peace Council, Colombo, Sri Lanka

Maria Småberg—PhD, Assistant Professor, Department of History, Lund University, Lund, Sweden

Preface

ONE OF THE MOST discussed themes in both domestic and international political arenas since the end of the Cold War has been the role of religion in politics: if religious actors or political actors with a religiously based agenda to an increasing degree have political ambitions, how does this affect conflicts as well as peace initiatives?

On the global level, and with some variations over time, there is on the whole a strong presence of religion, in history as well as in current life and culture. This makes religion—manifested as it is in thousands of forms—exposed and vulnerable, on the one hand, and powerful and attractive, on the other. Through their own institutions, religious actors can on the one hand play both a promoting and restraining role in relation to the use of violence and its justification. As a widespread social phenomenon, religion can—on the other hand—be used by anyone who wants moral support for his or her ideas, irrespective of the opinion of the allegedly supporting religion's majority or institutions.

Most observers would agree that religion plays a mixed role vis-a-vis politics. It can create conflict based on dogmatic and theoretical differences as well as identity and institutional connections. It can also restrain forces that prefer using violence to further an agenda, for instance through arguments based on what is a justifiable reason for war, and a justifiable conduct of war, if not proposing pacifism as a radical alternative to all too many compromises with violence. All these opinions are harbored within globally encompassing but locally worshipped religions.

This collection of studies on the connection between religion and armed conflict in a wide sense of the concept, brings perspective both on the promoting and restraining role of religion vis-a-vis violence, conflict, and conflict resolution. Its purpose is to illustrate the variety of approaches taken in the use of religion for a particular political cause, whether peaceful or not.

Not only the most recently discussed events and trends, with respect to religion and armed conflict, are represented in this collection. Some contributions have a clear anchorage in a historic process with ramifications until this day, and in which religion has played very different but fascinating roles.

This volume has its origin in cooperation on the theme of religion and conflict between three research institutions based in Uppsala, Sweden—the Church of Sweden Research Unit, the Life and Peace Institute, and the Department of Peace and Conflict Research, Uppsala University. Following institutional and staff changes, the volume was finalized with the inclusion also of Stockholm School of Theology, Stockholm, in the network.

Stockholm, September 2012
Kjell-Åke Nordquist

1

Religion, Fundamentalism, and Conflict

R. Scott Appleby

Since the event known as "9/11," when Islamic extremists piloted hijacked planes into the twin towers of the World Trade Center, New York, and the Pentagon, Washington DC (while a fourth hijacked airliner crashed in a Pennsylvania field), the fervent international debate about the roles of religion in deadly conflict has seen analysts gravitating toward one of two extremes. One camp follows in the tradition of religion's cultured despisers, pointing to the bogeyman of "fundamentalism" as evidence that religion is inherently opposed to every (liberal) expression of human freedom and committed to intolerant theocracy. To proponents of this approach to religious violence, "fundamentalism" is a catch-all term for a range of disparate phenomena, from any activity of religiously conservative or orthodox believers on the one hand, to religion-inflected wars and atrocities in conflict settings like the Balkans, Afghanistan, or Sri Lanka, on the other. To this camp—which equates religion, fundamentalism, and terrorism—absolutism, intolerance, and deadly violence is the true face of religion.

The other camp, which includes secular humanists who are friendly to organized religion, as well as many religious believers themselves, expects religion to uphold the humanist credo, including the proposition that human life is the highest good, the one inviolable reality. These proponents of enlightened religion tend to explain away acts of terrorism, murder, and sabotage committed in the name of religion: This is not Islam, this is not Christianity, this is not Sikhism, they contend, precisely

1

because the act and agents in question violate the sanctity of human life and dignity.[1]

The either/or method of analyzing religion—predicated on the assumption that one must decide whether religion is essentially a creative and "civilizing" force, on the one hand, or a destructive and inhumane specter from a benighted past, on the other—is no less prevalent for being patently absurd. Both positions on religion smack of reductionism. The cynics fail to appreciate the profoundly humane and humanizing attributes of religion and the moral constraints it imposes upon intolerant and violent behavior. The advocates of "liberalized" religion fail to consider that an authentic religious precept—a sincere response to the sacred—may end in subordinating human life to a higher good (e.g., unconditional obedience to God's law).[2]

Both of these camps hold a distorted view of religion, of fundamentalism, and of the relationship of each to armed conflict. Deconstructing the stereotypes they reinforce is the burden of this essay.

RELIGION: FLUID, ADAPTIVE, INTERNALLY PLURAL

People have believed in and practiced "religion" from the beginning of recorded history. Each community of belief and practice undertaken in response to the experience of the sacred has produced its own virtuosi and officials—priests, rabbis, ulema, gurus, and the like—who preside over sacred rituals and lead communal worship, proclaim doctrines, enforce ethical teachings, and organize the community.[3]

1. Appleby, *Ambivalence of the Sacred*, 10.

2. Ibid.

3. The "objective" and comparative study of religion as a phenomenon found in every society is less than two hundred years old, however. The Western Enlightenment, the sweeping cultural and intellectual movement that elevated reason over revelation in the eighteenth century, led to the separation of scientific inquiry from religious belief. An important legacy of the Enlightenment is the idea that religion is a human enterprise or product, much like politics or culture, with its own inner dynamics and rules that can be examined rather than experienced as a gift from God. By the dawn of the twentieth century religion itself had become an object of scholarly or "scientific" study. Since then, the study of religion in the West has been conducted mostly by scholars who do not share the perspectives and beliefs of the people they study. Journalists as well as scholars have adopted an increasingly detached and analytical view of religion. Their approach has tended to minimize the unique nature of religious experience and behaviors. It views religion not as an independent reality, but as a colorful, dramatic, and often violent expression of "something else"—of political, social, economic, or psychological needs or desires, for example. See Capps, *Religious Studies*.

To various degrees the great religious traditions, in their teach-ings and commentaries on the sacred scriptures and doctrines, evolved hermeneutics, or interpretive strategies, designed to identify the sacred more and more completely with its benevolent, life-giving aspect. In the Traditions of the Book—Judaism, Christianity, and Islam—God is the ultimate source of the Good, the True, and the Beautiful; Satan, the de-structive aspect of the numinous, is banished from the godhead. These traditions vary significantly, of course, both in comparison to one anoth-er and within themselves, as to the credence they continue to give to the primordial notion of divine wrath and retribution. In Eastern traditions such as Buddhism and Hinduism, ambivalence reigns colorfully in the mundane religious imagination, where avatars of fertility commingle with warrior gods. Enlightenment, however, is a state of transcendence beyond a world imprisoned in these illusionary dualisms.

Within each of these great traditions, notwithstanding their profound substantive differences, one can trace a moral trajectory challenging adherents to greater acts of compassion, forgiveness and reconciliation, and delegitimating as "demonic" the competing voices of revenge and retaliation that continue to claim the status of authentic religious expression. It is this internal evolution of the great religious traditions that commands our attention, for these traditions spawn the most significant religio-political movements of our time, from the vio-lent extremist cadres to the organizations of faith-based peacemakers. Thus it behooves us to understand how change occurs within these reli-gions, how spin-off movements form to advocate and embody different elements within these internally plural and ambiguous traditions, and how external actors and circumstances influence both processes.

In striving to adhere to traditional beliefs and moral codes, reli-gious actors recognize that tradition is pluriform and cumulative, de-veloped in and for concrete and changing situations. Decisions based on religious principles reflect the ways religious authorities interpret and apply the received tradition in specific circumstances. In this process the *internal pluralism* of any religious tradition—the multiplicity of its teachings, images of the divine, moral injunctions, and so on—bestows upon the religious leader the power of choice. It falls inevitably to the evangelist, prophet, rabbi, priest, sage, religious scholar or guru to select the appropriate doctrine or norm in a given situation and thus to define what is orthodox or heretical, moral or immoral, permitted or forbidden, at a particular moment.[4]

Gaps between dogma and ideology—or, to put it differently, between professed belief and operative belief—are found in every religion and historical period. This alone does not constitute a betrayal of religious ideals. Religious traditions are inherently dynamic, composed of what Cardinal Newman called "leading ideas," which interact with "a multitude of opinions" and introduce themselves into "the framework and details of social life."[5]

Religious traditions can adapt to their environments without eroding continuity with the sacred past because the past is capacious. The notion of "internal pluralism" suggests an array of laws, doctrines, moral norms, and "practices" (socially imbedded beliefs) sacralized and sanctioned at various times by the community and its religious authorities. This storehouse of religiously approved options is available to religious leaders whenever new circumstances call for change in religious practice. Scientific developments, for example, may transform the believer's understanding of the world and shift the context for moral decision-making, thereby providing justification for ransacking the religious past.

The philosopher Alasdair MacIntyre defines a "living tradition" as "an historically extended, socially embodied argument, and an argument precisely in part about the goods which constitute that tradition."[6] MacIntyre's formulation, coupled with Newman's notion of religious "ideas" awaiting development in each historical period, suggest a working definition of a "religious tradition" as a sustained argument, conducted anew by each generation, about the contemporary significance and meaning of the sources of sacred wisdom and revealed truth (i.e., sacred scriptures, oral and written commentaries, authoritative teachings, etc.). The argument alternately recapitulates, ignores, and moves beyond old debates, but draws on the same sacred sources as did previous generations of believers. It follows its own inner logic and rules, and generates distinctive patterns of thought and action. According to MacIntyre, the argument is "precisely in part about the goods which

---

4. Appleby, *Ambivalence of the Sacred*, 31–32.

5. Newman, *An Essay on the Development*, 35, 37–38.

6. MacIntyre, *After Virtue*, 204–5; see also Appleby, *Ambivalence of the Sacred*, 33.

constitute that tradition"—and in part about the practices which sustain and extend those goods to the individual and the community.[7]

What is striking about the recent past is that the religious "argument" has unfolded in Christianity and Judaism, in Islam and Hinduism and Sikhism, around the notion that these historic traditions are under siege, threatened to their very core, by irreligious or corrupt religious forces and trends linked to the rise of secular modernity. Strikingly, there has emerged within each of these religious traditions a comparable "logic"—a modern mode of political religiosity that justifies, embraces and elaborates a militant reaction to the religious and secular "other." This religious logic has come to be known as "fundamentalism."

FUNDAMENTALISM: SELECTIVE, REACTIVE, ABSOLUTIST, DUALIST, APOCALYPTIC

The Western media began to take special notice of the violent, "uncivilized" dimensions of religion in the 1970s. Observers pointed to the rise of the politically influential New Christian Right in the United States, the messianic ideas of Jews who settled the occupied territories of the West Bank and Gaza in hopes of extending Israel's boundaries to "Biblical proportions," and the violent activism of certain Sunni Muslim groups. The most powerful cause of the media's fascination with religion's "dark side," however, was the Islamic Revolution in Iran (1978–1979), which shocked U.S. and European policy makers and intellectuals who had presumed that religion was a spent force in the modern world. How, astonished reporters and politicians wondered, could a "medieval" ayatollah transform a supposedly secularizing nation like Iran into a semi-theocracy (a nation ruled by religious law and clergy)? After all, Iran under the Shah had been moving away from religious identity and religious justifications for its public policies, foreign alignments, and economic practices.

By the mid-1980s the world seemed to be on fire with "radical religion." The government of India, supported by militant Hindu nationalists who promoted India as a "Hindu nation," were fighting Sikh separatists of the Punjab, who employed their own brand of deadly violence in an ultimately futile effort to secede from India. "Buddhist nationalism" colored the civil war between Sinhalese and Tamils in Sri Lanka. In the

---

7. MacIntyre, *After Virtue*, 222.

Holy Land of the Middle East Jewish messianists of the religious settler movement Gush Emunim clashed lethally with Sunni Muslim extremists of the Palestinian Muslim resistance movement Hamas. In failed states such as Lebanon and Afghanistan, Muslim "freedom fighters" (such as Lebanon's Shi'ite movement, Hezbollah—"the Party of God") attempted to establish Muslim sovereignty over the state.

Although these groups had little in common and were not co-operating with one another, American journalists and some scholars lumped them together. They reached back for a familiar word—"fundamentalism"—to describe the phenomenon. "Fundamentalism" was first used by evangelical Christians of the 1910s and 1920s who proclaimed themselves willing to wage "battle royal" for "the fundamentals of the faith."[8] In the 1980s, journalists began to extend the term "fundamentalism" well beyond its original North American context, to militant Sikh, Muslim, Jewish, and Buddhist groups. The term is in many ways an unfortunate one, however, because its frequent misuse and promiscuous application lead some people to conclude that all seriously committed religious people are fundamentalists, and that all fundamentalists are a public menace. Nonetheless, numerous scholarly and popular studies of "global fundamentalism" and religious violence were published in the 1980s and 1990s.[9]

8. Appleby and Marty, *Fundamentalisms Observed*, 2.

9. From 1988 to 1993 the American Academy of Arts and Sciences devoted the funding from a major public policy grant to "The Fundamentalism Project," a comparative study of worldwide religious resurgence, political religion and religiously motivated violence. Seventy-five scholars from twenty nations contributed to the project, which produced five encyclopedic scholarly volumes published by the University of Chicago Press and edited by Martin E. Marty and R. Scott Appleby. Several spin-off books and essays also appeared, including *Islamic Fundamentalisms and the Gulf Crisis*, translated into several languages worldwide, and *Spokesmen for the Despised*, a collection of biographical profiles of "fundamentalist" leaders of the Middle East. The literature on religious conflict and religious violence has grown significantly over the past twenty years, with innumerable titles published after 9/11. Among the most influential authors are Mark Juergensmeyer (*Terror in the Mind of God: The Global Rise of Religious Violence*, 2000), Gilles Kepel (*Jihad: The Trail of Political Islam*, 2002) and Philip Jenkins (*The Next Christendom: The Coming of Global Christianity*, 2002). In 1994, the sociologist of religion José Casanova wrote an influential book, *Public Religion in the Modern World* (University of Chicago Press), that scolded Western scholars and academics for underestimating the resilience of religion in national and international affairs. Casanova noted that most Western observers of the worldwide "resurgence of religion" had assumed that the world was becoming completely secularized or devoid of religion. Thus they were taken completely by surprise by the "news" that religions remain quite

The themes and findings of these studies are too numerous to be summarized fully, but a few should be mentioned here. First, members of these religious movements fear or hate the modern nation-state. The modern state, they argue, is godless and therefore morally and spiritually bankrupt. It regulates many aspects of social existence and establishes the basic political and cultural conditions within which social life occurs. Thus, "fundamentalist" religious actors often feel compelled to provide a strong religious alternative or challenge to the state. Even when fundamentalists attempt to preserve their separateness from secular society, however, they find themselves participating in a common discourse about modernization, development, political structures, and economic planning.

Second, most of these movements are composed of religious believers who chose to separate from their orthodox or traditionalist communities. People of religious consciousness and conscience are being pushed to the margins of society, they believe. Accordingly, "true believers" must "fight back" against nonbelievers and "lukewarm" believers. In this context, male charismatic or authoritarian leaders emerged from each religious tradition, often in defiance of the conventional religious leadership. These new leaders ransacked the tradition's past, retrieving and restoring politically useful doctrines and practices, and creating others. They were successful in creating an ideology that mobilized disgruntled youth into militant cadres or into grassroots political organizations. The religious militants established new boundaries between "insiders" and "outsiders" and imposed a strict discipline on their followers. In many cases, they were able to elevate their mission to a spiritual plane in which apocalyptic, or "end-times" urgency informed even the most mundane tasks of the group.

Third, all of this unfolded in the name of defending and preserving a cherished collective identity rooted in religious tradition. Strikingly, most of these movements did not look backward but forward. They look to the past for inspiration rather than for a blueprint. Direction and models for reform of society came not only from a selective interpretation of the sacred past, but also from imitation of what works in

---

capable of causing or extending deadly conflicts. No one doubts that truth now. But most scholars of politics and culture, as well as practitioners of conflict resolution, are still learning that religion can also be a powerful source of conflict prevention, management, and resolution.

the present—including what works for the modern state! Thus militant religious actors became important players in local, regional and even national politics, not as a result of their nostalgia or "backwardness," but as a result of their ability to adapt to modern organizational imperatives, political strategies, communications advances, and economic theories.

When fundamentalists react to the marginalization of religion, that is, they do so as modern people formed in a pluralist, secular milieu. They might invoke the pristine moment of origin of the Davidic kingdom or Christendom or Islamic civilization, but the fundamentalists are looking ahead, not backward. Educated and formed epistemologically under the banner of techno-scientific modernity, most "middle-managers" of fundamentalist movements are trained as engineers, software experts, medical technicians, soldiers, politicians, teachers, and bureaucrats. They are pragmatists of the soul. Few are astrophysicists or speculative philosophers. Stinger missiles, modern media, airliners, and cyberspace are their milieu. They have little patience and no time for the ambiguities of the vast, multivalent religious tradition.

Given their emergence from the heart of secular modernity, these would-be defenders of traditional religion approach the scriptures and traditions as an architect reads a blueprint, or an engineer scans his toolbox: they plumb the sacred sources for the instruments appropriate to the task. By this habit they reveal themselves to be modern, not traditional. In competition with the "Westoxicated" moderns, the fundamentalists select, mix and match, recombine, innovate, create, build. They grow impatient and angry with mere traditionalists, who insist on disciplining themselves to the tradition as an organic, mysterious, non-linear, irreducible, life-giving whole. There is no time for such luxuries, such refinements, as the fundamentalists implore: we are *at war*, our souls as well as lives depend on swift and powerful retaliation: this is *urgent!*

And so the mode of reaction to the marginalization of religion is, ironically, fundamentally modern, instrumental, rational—and manipulative of the religious tradition.

Thus fundamentalists, whether vaguely or explicitly aware of the compromises they are compelled to make, practice *selective retrieval* not only of aspects of secular modernity, but also of the host religion. From the religious sensibility they choose the elements most resistant to relativism, pluralism, and other concomitants of secular modernity that conspire to reduce the autonomy and hegemony of the religious. Hence fundamentalists embrace *absolutism* and *dualism* as tactics of resistance, and as justification for extremism in the service of a sacred cause.

In an attempt to protect the holy book or hallowed tradition from the depredations of historical, literary, and scientific criticism—that is, from criteria of validity and ways of knowing that deny the transcendence of the sacred—fundamentalist leaders claim *inerrancy* and *infallibility* for their religious knowledge. The truth revealed in scriptures and hallowed traditions is neither contingent nor variable, but absolute. To underscore the trans-rational (and thus counter-modern) nature of absolute truth, each movement selects from its host religion certain scandalous doctrines (i.e., beliefs not easily reconcilable to scientific rationality, such as the imminent return of the Hidden Imam, the literal virgin birth of Christ, the divinity of the Lord Ram, the coming of the Messiah to restore and rule "the Whole Land of Israel"). These "supernatural dicta" they embellish, reify, and politicize.

The confession of literal belief in these hard-to-swallow "fundamentals" sets the self-described true believers apart from the Westoxicated masses. Moreover, it marks them as members of a sacred remnant, an elect tribe commissioned to defend the sacred against an array of "reprobate," "fallen" and "polluted" co-religionists—and against the forces of evil that have corrupted the religious community. This *dualist* or Manichean worldview valorizes the children of light, in stark contrast to the children of darkness, and reinforces the fundamentalists' conviction that they are specially chosen by God to withstand the forces of irreligion.

Yet a reliance on absolutism and dualism as a mode of selective reaction to the marginalization of religion is not enough. The leaders and organizers of these reactive and selective religious movements typically are drawn toward extremism, that is, toward extralegal, often violent measures to realize a meaningful victory over their enemies. But they have a recruiting problem, for their pool of potential disciples is drawn not only from the religiously illiterate and untutored or drifting youth, but more centrally from conservative and orthodox believers—people who are familiar with their scriptures, embrace the tradition in its complexity and recognize that it enjoins compassion and mercy toward others, not intolerance, hatred, and violence. Theoretically at least, violence and retaliation are not the only strategies for resisting evil. Separatism or passive resistance might suffice to withstand the encroachments of the world. Guerrilla war, terrorism, and the killing of innocents seem a breathtakingly severe and indeed unorthodox reaction.

This is why *millennialism* is the ideological characteristic that stands at the heart of the religious logic of fundamentalism. It is also the trait that sets contemporary religious violence in the fundamentalist mode apart from other types of revolutionary or terrorist violence by resistance or oppositional movements. Indeed, the specific contours, timing, and purposes of fundamentalist violence are dictated by this aspect of the religious imagination, which fundamentalists amplify and turn to their particular political ends.

"Millennialism," as it is used here, is an umbrella term encompassing the full array of "apocalyptic," "eschatological," or "end-times" doctrines, myths and precepts embedded in the history and religious imagination of the major religious traditions of the world. Islam, Christianity and Judaism, for example, all anticipate a dramatic moment in time, or beyond time, in which God will bring history to a just (and often bloody) culmination. In certain religious communities, such as Shi'ite Islam or evangelical Protestant Christianity, this expectation is highly pronounced and developed. (Indeed, the term "millennialism," when used precisely, refers to the prophesied 1,000-year reign of the Christ, following his return in glory to defeat the Anti-Christ.) What is striking, however, is the recent retrieval of "millennial" (or messianic or apocalyptic or eschatological) themes, images, and myths by fundamentalists from religious communities with a muted or underdeveloped strain of "end times" thought.[10]

How does this retrieval and embellishment of apocalyptic or millennial themes function within fundamentalist movements that seek recruits from among their orthodox co-religionists? Leaders seeking to form cadres for jihad or crusade or anti-Muslim (or anti-Jewish, etc.) riots must convince the religiously literate fellow believer that violence is justified in religious terms. Luckily for them, most scriptures and traditions contain ambiguities and exceptions—including what might be called "emergency clauses." Thus the Granth Sahib, the holy book and living guru of the Sikhs, repeatedly enjoins forgiveness, compassion and love toward enemies. It does, however, also contain an injunction calling believers to arms, if necessary, if the Sikh religion itself is threatened with extinction—a passage put to use by Jarnail Singh Bhindranwale,

10. Freyer Stowasser, *A Time to Reap.*

the Sikh militant who cut a swath of terror through the Punjab in the early 1980s. Such "emergency clauses" can be found in the Qur'an, the Hebrew Bible, and the New Testament as well. And what better "emergency" than the advent of the predicted "dark age" or reign of evil that precedes the coming of the Messiah, the return of the Mahdi, the vindication of the righteous at God's hands?

The fundamentalist invocation of "millennialism," in short, strives to convince believers that they are engaged not merely in a mundane struggle for territory or political power or financial gain, but in a "cosmic war," a battle for the soul and for the future of humanity.[11] In such a context, violence is not only permissible; it is obligatory.

FUNDAMENTALISM AND ARMED CONFLICT

Not all fundamentalist movements endorse or employ violence: some are morally opposed to killing, while others are constrained by a powerful state and law enforcement agencies. Yet numerous such movements and individuals who feel threatened by the seemingly all-powerful secular nation-state, or by fellow believers who have compromised with it, see conflict as inevitable and violence as a religious duty. Nothing is more important than fulfilling the will of God, as proclaimed in sacred texts and religious laws, and as interpreted (by charismatic religious leaders) through the lens of contemporary events.

Fulfilling God's will may require sacrificing lives in the struggle to regain or possess land considered sacred. Thus, Jewish as well as Muslim radicals risk or offer their lives for control of sacred sites in Jerusalem; and Hindus and Muslims fight to the death for contested land in Ayodhya, India, where in 1993 a major mosque was destroyed by Hindu nationalists seeking to avenge what they saw as the desecration of the birthplace of the Lord Ram. Serving a divine cause may entail driving the U.S. army from Iraq or expelling Russian forces form Chechnya, just as Muslim mujahideen drove the Soviets from Afghanistan. Or, it may mean that Iranian mothers must send their children across minefields, in the effort to unseat Saddam Hussein, the great persecutor of Shi'ite Muslims of southern Iraq—as they did during the Iran-Iraq war of the 1980s. For some Christians, obeying God means ending abortion by any means necessary, including the killing of doctors.

---

11. On "cosmic war," see Juergensmeyer, *Terror in the Mind of God*, 145–63.

Within the logic of fundamentalism, that is, one discovers a trajectory toward violence and war. The bracing complexity of religious reactions and the diversity of options even with the fundamentalist mode of religiosity means, however, that not all fundamentalists will follow this trajectory to its culmination and actually engage in terrorist violence or armed conflict. Accordingly, the central theoretical questions include the following: *What imposes constraints on fundamentalist violence— that is, what factors or conditions inhibit fundamentalists from expressing their resistance and reaction through armed aggression? Conversely, under what conditions is fundamentalist violence and armed aggression likely to occur?*

Theorizing in response to these questions is now possible, in light of the body of research, including independent case studies, that has accumulated over several decades. Systematic analysis of these cases indicates that the nature of the state—its level of militarization, on the one hand, and the space and autonomy it allows to civil society, on the other, is the decisive structural condition that creates the conditions of possibility for the growth and development of fundamentalist movements—and also for their resort to violence or armed conflict, in the settings where this occurs. Similarly, "the nature of the state" is the most important factor in predicting the suppression or moderation of fundamentalist extremism.[12]

---

12. A quarter-century of reports on suicide bombers, the Religious Right, Al-Qaeda, the Taliban and "militant" Burmese monks (all of whom have been described as "fundamentalists") bear out the need to differentiate between logics. In an indirect acknowledgment of the fundamentalists' technological and political savvy, the post-9/11 flood of polemics against Islamists (sometimes equated with all Muslims) takes a tone of awed alarm, not condescension. For example, an "exposé" of Tariq Ramadan by the French feminist editor of *ProChoix*, "an anti-racist and anti-fundamentalist journal and website," finds the Swiss Muslim intellectual a daunting adversary precisely because he is "urbane," "articulate," and "ingenious," a thoroughly sophisticated modern philosopher "who claims to be attached to secularism, even if he wants to see it evolve."

Even more destabilizing to the received wisdom regarding fundamentalists—the "here be monsters" attitude toward them—is the lack of any sound study or other evidence that persuasively links fundamentalists, or the so-called "fundamentalist mindset," to a type of mental illness or emotional pathology such as "the authoritarian personality"—and this absence of hard evidence is certainly not for lack of trying. Nor do fundamentalists, despite still being repeatedly depicted as brutally violent, enjoy a monopoly on extralegal political violence, torture, or systematic violation of human rights, as polemics against the second Bush administration, the Musharraf regime, or other state-centered violators of international law and human rights norms make clear.

Two relational patterns tend to affect the fundamentalists' resort to armed conflict, and their success in waging it when they attempt to do so. One pattern is a military regime or police state where all dissent is ruthlessly crushed by direct application of force, and/or where voluntary organizations, oppositional political parties, labor syndicates, religious groups and other expressions of civil society are tightly controlled and manipulated by the regime. Syria is an example of the former, while Egypt combines elements of both approaches.

The other form of governance that impedes fundamentalist resort to armed conflict is a vibrant democracy with a robust civil society, where pluralism flourishes, individual rights are protected, and the rule of law is enforced by a competent state. In such settings fundamentalist movements tend not to fight to the death, but rather seek to increase their portion of the political and resource pie, to expand their recruiting reach and, ultimately, to "transform the world" through political and cultural agency rather than armed conflict.[13] This pattern is illustrated by the history of the New Christian Right in the United States, the Jammat-i-Islami in Pakistan, and the various political incarnations of the Islamist movement in Turkey, including The Justice and Development Party, or AKP, the political party in power at this writing.[14]

Examination of the development of such movements over time indicates that fundamentalism is not a static condition or a consistently violent expression of the "essence" of the host religion in question. To the contrary, fundamentalism—best understood as a mode of politicized religion and religiosity—is subject to the same dynamics that condition both religion and politics. As we have seen, religion is a fluid, internally plural, shifting and adapting reality that exists in continual interaction with its specific social, political, and cultural environment. Politics, especially as practiced in a globalized, pluralist milieu, is the art of compromise and continual negotiation, punctuated by the rhythms of resistance and accommodation. The religio-political movements known as "fundamentalisms" are hardly immune from these dynamics. Indeed,

13. Almond, Appleby, and Sivan, *Strong Religion*, 168–79.

14. The Justice and Development Party or White Party (Turkish: Adalet ve Kalkż nma Partisi or AK Parti, or AKPÝ, is the incumbent Turkish political party. The AKP portrays itself as a moderate, conservative, pro-Western party that advocates a liberal market economy and Turkish membership in the European Union. Abdullah Gül, a prominent AKP leader and former Foreign Minister, is currently the President of Turkey, while Recep Tayyip Erdoğan is the head of the party and the Prime Minister.

the evidence indicates that fundamentalism in the late twentieth and early twenty-first century is a mode of religious politics (and politicized religion) that is available to social protest movements across the globe.[15] The movements that inhabit this mode follow a certain logic, outlined above, characterized by reaction, selective retrieval of tradition and appropriation of techno-scientific instrumentalism, uncompromising absolutism, demonizing dualism, and violence-justifying "millennialism."

Because fundamentalism is an available logic, a mode of social protest, rather than a static condition, movements can and often do move in and out of this mode. "Pure fundamentalism," so to speak, is a temporary and indeed increasingly rare mode of operation, given the enormous pressures upon social protest movements to leave their constructed enclaves, engage outsiders, temper demonizing rhetoric, and adopt a position of moderation and political compromise. When religious actors choose, instead, to engage in armed conflict, whether by waging war or conducting terrorist operations, the fundamentalist mode is readily available. Indeed, the most striking expressions of fundamentalism are those multi-generational movements—Gush Emunim in Israel, U.S. Christian fundamentalism, the Muslim Brotherhood, etc.—which have maintained an oppositional, defiant, and absolutist stance across several decades. But even these "fundamentalisms" have engaged in armed conflict only intermittently, and then to various degrees of intensity and coordination.

BIBLIOGRAPHY

Almond, Gabriel A., R. Scott Appleby, and Emmanuel Sivan. *Strong Religion: The Rise of Fundamentalisms Around the World.* Chicago: University of Chicago Press, 2003.

Appleby, R. Scott. *The Ambivalence of the Sacred: Religion, Violence and Reconciliation.* Lanham: Rowman & Littlefield, 2000.

Appleby, R. Scott, ed. *Spokesmen for the Despised.* Chicago: University of Chicago Press, 1997.

Capps, Walter. *Religious Studies: The Making of a Discipline.* Minneapolis: Fortress, 1995.

Casanova, José. *Public Religion in the Modern World.* Chicago: University of Chicago Press, 1994.

Freyer Stowasser, Barbara. "A Time to Reap." *Middle East Studies Association Bulletin* 34/1 (Summer 2000) 1–13.

Jenkins, Philip. *The Next Christendom: The Coming of Global Christianity.* Oxford: Oxford University Press, 2002.

15. Almond, Appleby, and Sivan, *Strong Religion*, 168–79.

Juergensmeyer, Mark. *Terror in the Mind of God: The Global Rise of Religious Violence.* Berkely: University of California Press, 2000.

Kepel, Gilles. *Jihad: The Trail of Political Islam.* London: Tauris, 2002.

MacIntyre, Alasdair. *After Virtue: A Study in Moral Theory.* Notre Dame: University of Notre Dame Press, 1991.

Marty, Martin E., and R. Scott Appleby, eds. *Fundamentalisms Observed.* Chicago: University of Chicago Press, 1991.

Newman, John Henry. *An Essay on the Development of Christian Doctrine.* Notre Dame: University of Notre Dame Press, 1989.

Piscatori, James, ed. *Islamic Fundamentalisms and the Gulf Crisis.* Chicago: Fundamentalism Project, 1991.

2

Religion in the Global Jihadi War

MARK JUERGENSMEYER

"This is war," a Sunni Muslim cleric told me in Baghdad.[1] He was not talking about the initial attack by U.S. forces that brought down Saddam Hussein's regime, but about the resistance struggle throughout Iraq more than a year later. In a curious way, the full force of war came home to him and many of his compatriots in Iraq months after the U.S.-led military coalition that invaded Iraq in April 2003—an event that those who supported the coalition called the liberation of the country, and that many Iraqis considered the beginning of American occupation.

The resistance was a war against America. But it was not necessarily a war in favor of Saddam Hussein. The Sunni cleric with whom I spoke had hated Saddam. The cleric told me that members of his own family had been killed by the dictator, and he was happy to see Saddam leave. Yet curiously the cleric had little appreciation for the coalition military forces that brought Saddam down.

As the months lengthened into years, the cleric's anger over the U.S. military presence festered into hatred. As the Fallujah insurgency gained strength his feelings crystallized into a view of war. He saw the U.S. forces as an ultimate enemy, hell-bent on destroying Iraqi society and Muslim culture. Increasingly he became persuaded of the merits of the jihadi rhetoric. He began to accept the idea that the U.S. was in Iraq

1. Interview with Sheik Muhammad al-Kubaisi.

16

in order to subjugate and destroy Islam. What else, he asked me, could explain the persistence of the U.S. presence and the humiliating way in which he and other Iraqis were treated. He felt that even the sacrifice of life was warranted in destroying them. It was a war that he could not imagine losing. It was a sacred struggle, the ultimate war.

It is a remarkable notion, the idea of war. It came over Iraq like a cloud that poisoned the process of peaceful transition to a democratic state. It descended into the thinking and attitudes of Iraqis months after the end of the initial assault—after the battles of the invasion were over, and after Americans had congratulated themselves on "a job well done." Gradually the idea insinuated itself into the minds of many average Iraqis who began to see the American-led coalition forces as more than just an irritating occupying presence. They began to see them as enemies in a global war.

Yet their image of warfare was, in an interesting way, the mirror response to the fervor of patriotic militancy that brought U.S. troops to Iraq in the first place. The flag that an American soldier had draped over the face of the statute of Saddam Hussein that was toppled in Fardus Square on that celebrated moment during the U.S. capture of Baghdad on April 9, 2003 had flown over the Pentagon on the fateful day of September 11, 2001. The flag was only briefly on Saddam's sculptured face before the soldier's superiors, realizing it could have adverse public relations effects, made him remove it. The young soldier, U.S. Marine First Lieutenant Tim McLaughlin said he knew that Saddam had nothing to do with the attack on the Pentagon and World Trade Center, but placing the flag there made him feel better.[2] He felt that toppling a bad leader in the Middle East, even if it was not Osama bin Laden, somehow helped to even the score.

This sense of patriotic war fervor that was elicited by the September 11 attacks was, in turn, a reflection of the extremist Muslim martial furor that motivated those who perpetrated the awful events of that day. Few, if any, of the thousands who lost their lives when the Twin Towers in New York collapsed were leaders of American power. Yet one of the men involved in plotting the 1993 attack on the World Trade Center told me that office buildings such as this were chosen as targets to show that the economic and military power of the U.S. was vulnerable. "There is a war going on," Mahmud Abouhalima told me when I interviewed

2. Quoted in the *Times of London*, April 11, 2003.

him in prison, years after the 1993 attack.[3] It was a war that, in his telling, the U.S. had initiated. The Muslim world had become victimized by American power, he said, and now Americans were beginning to feel the agony that he claimed that he and his compatriots had felt for many years.

The wheel of warfare had come full circle. The simmering resentment over American power and influence in the Muslim world had crystallized into a sense of warfare. A decade of sporadic jihadi terrorist attacks finally struck home on September 11, 2001—or rather September 12, when Americans, in response, adopted the jihadi worldview and also began to see the world at war. The sense of urgency that led to the immediate military action in Afghanistan after the September 11 attacks persisted, and the public's gnawing feelings of fear about a vague international threat became a major element in the popular support for the invasion of Iraq. That invasion and the excesses of American occupation that followed provided fuel for the fires of Muslim extremism throughout the Middle East, turning Iraq into a theater of jihadi war.

How did this come to pass? Why did this way of thinking about the world—a world embroiled in war—seem so natural, so inevitable, so appealing, on both sides?

A NEW WAR

By the middle of the first decade of the twenty-first century it became clear that in the mindset of many people the world was confronting a new war. It was a global war, one characterized by terrorism and the response to it. It did not arrive with a name, at least not a single one. Wars do not find a commonly accepted name until often years later when the frequency of usage provides an appellation that can be linked to them. The global conflict of the first decade of the twenty-first century was a war that was described differently depending on one's point of view.

From the perspective of one of the conflict's protagonists, Osama bin Laden, it was a war against infidels and crusaders. In his 1996 fatweh pronouncing a war against the United States, bin Laden stated that "the crusader forces became the main cause of our disastrous condition," explaining that they had destroyed Saudi Arabia and the Middle East eco-

---

3. Interview with Mahmud Abouhalima.

nomically, politically, and culturally.[4] So perhaps from a radical Islamic perspective it could be called the New Crusader War.

From the perspective of bin Laden's nemesis, U.S. President George W. Bush, it was a "global war on terror." The September 11 attack on the World Trade Center and the Pentagon was deemed "an act of war" by the President in his first televised speech to the nation the afternoon of the attacks. On the next day he inaugurated the phrase, "the war on terror." It continued for years to frame the way the U.S. response to the attacks was characterized and it anchored the foreign policy that led to the invasion and occupation of Iraq. In July 2005, at a time when opinion polls showed the American public increasingly disenchanted with the war in Iraq and less enthusiastic about the President's leadership in foreign affairs in general, the Bush administration quietly dropped "the war on terrorism" appellation and began to speak instead about the "global struggle against radical Islam." In the administration of President Barack Obama that followed George W. Bush, the phrase was dropped completely. Still, the idea of a global terror war had been deeply impressed on the American consciousness, and for many Americans that term continued to symbolize the bellicose atmosphere of the post-September 11 world.

One could, however, search for a more neutral language and adopt Samuel Huntington's prescient phrase in his 1993 article in *Foreign Affairs* in which he prophetically questioned the arrival of a "clash of civilizations."[5] Some have argued, however, that Huntington's phrase placed too much emphasis on the differences among cultures rather than the political positions of extreme ideologues. According to these critiques, there is nothing inherently oppositional between Islam and the values of the European Enlightenment. To cast the global conflict in civilizational terms is to accept bin Laden's characterization of the struggle. Those who thought in terms of a clash of civilizations were accused of abandoning moderate Islam. To the extent that the use of the phrase enlarged tensions between Muslims and non-Muslims it became a self-fulfilling prophecy. The war terminology could create a war mentality.

In fact, this is true of any use of the word "war." I have hesitated to use this term to describe the response to terrorism for just this reason, since any encouragement of the use of the term "war" to talk about

---

4. Bin Laden, "Declaration of War Against the Americans."

5. Huntington, "The Clash of Civilizations?"

the situation could imply support for the bellicose thinking behind it and help to bring about even greater possibilities for violence. iIn most heated encounters, the warlike attitudes on both sides of the conflict are unnecessary exaggerations of the differences between them. To think in terms of war is to make irreconcilable the positions that could conceivably find common ground. Yet we cannot ignore what was in fact the case: a warring mood that in the first decade of the twenty-first century descended into the public imaginations of segments of both the Muslim and Western worlds. It dominated the news media—not just the more ideological media, like Fox News (U.S.) and Al Jazeera (Qatar), but also the many news services that thought of themselves as neutral, such as CNN and *The New York Times*. And the idea of war influenced the foreign policies of the United States, Great Britain, and their allies. We cannot deny that this attitude of war existed. The only question is how to make sense of it.

The search for understanding this war worldview begins with our description of it. A "clash of civilizations" unnecessarily brands the whole of the Muslim world against the West. The "terror war" phrase is less likely to be interpreted as a war on Islam, but the word "terror" is problematic in other ways.

For a time I thought that the simplest way of describing the current conflict was to call it "the global terror war." But the more I thought about it, I thought that this term would miss the point. It would fixate on a tactic rather than on an issue, and thereby hinder our attempt to understand the situation. Though the term "terror" couched the conflict in a way that Americans and Europeans could easily understand, most Muslim activists who supported the jihadi cause would find "terror" to be an inadequate way of portraying what the conflict was about and why it was waged in such a violent manner. What they would take umbrage at is the notion that the illicit violence associated with the word "terror" comes only from their side. The point that Abouhalima made in my prison interview with him was that the Americans, in his view, started the fight. He claimed that the violence created by American military, economic, political, and cultural domination of the Middle East was the cause of the problem and that his own violence in attempting to bring down the World Trade Center—even though it appeared to most Americans as terrorism—was simply a response.

We might not agree with his assessment of the situation—few Americans or Europeans would—but it is important to take seriously the activists' point of view in order to understand the problem. As much as we might hate what they have done and despise them and their cause, to make sense of the conflict we have to see the world from their point of view. Understanding a war requires us to enter into the mindset of both sides. The old adage of "knowing one's enemy" applies. For many who are baffled by the war language and are perplexed about how the state of global relationships has reached this impasse, it is a matter of trying to understand the other's perspective.

For these reasons I have rejected the term "terror," and settled on the name, "the Global Jihadi War." It was global in that it was sparked with confrontations on virtually every continent, from Bali to Madrid, from Sharm el-Shaik to New York City. Scarcely a country in the world was untouched by the concerns of security and public violence that this conflict raised. It was a conflict in which the jihadi rhetoric was central—both to those radical Muslims who saw Western power as their enemy as well as to those who launched a "war on terrorism" against them. It is interesting in this regard that when the Bush administration decided to drop the "terror war" appellation in July 2005 it was the "struggle against radical Islam" that was the preferred alternative. The jihadi perspective was still the enemy. Yet even after July 2005 it was not just a "struggle" that the U.S. was undertaking—too many countries were terrorized and invaded and too many lives were lost for that term to correctly describe the mood of those who were engaged in the conflict. Clearly, from both sides' perspectives, it was war.

By 2011, the Global Jihadi War was largely over. When Barack Obama succeeded George W. Bush in 2009, the "war on terror" terminology was almost immediately abandoned. The symbolic transition in U.S. foreign policy came when President Obama traveled to Cairo on June 4, 2009, to give a speech focusing on U.S. reconciliation with the Muslim world. The two wars in Iraq and Afghanistan lingered on, but in December 18, 2011, the last active soldiers in the U.S. military left the country, and the war was officially over. In 2012, the U.S. actively negotiated with the Taliban to conclude the Afghan conflict. Earlier in 2011, on May 2, an elite cadre of U.S. Navy Seals stole into Osama bin Laden's secret compound in Abbottabad, Pakistan and killed the jihadi leader. But perhaps the most decisive strike against the jihadi ideology came with the Arab Spring uprisings across the Arab world in 2011 when popular uprisings against entrenched political regimes in the Muslim world appeared to be more efficient than sporadic acts of religious terrorism. By 2012 the Global Jihadi War seemed to be largely a thing of the past, though remnants of the ideology that provoked it, the terrorism that ignited it, and the extreme military and political measures that were invoked in response to it, all lingered on.

How important was this war in world affairs? This is something that time will tell and historians will assess. But it could well be considered to have been World War IV—following World War I, World War II, and the Cold War. In its all-encompassing warfare and in the starkly dichotomous way that each side viewed the other, the Global Jihadi War became a successor to the great international conflicts of the twentieth century. This is the point of view adopted in an analysis of U.S. foreign policy by Andrew Bacevich, who proclaimed that what I am calling the Global Jihadi War was indeed a new world war.[6] By Bacevich's calculation, the Cold War was by all accounts a world war, one that certainly equaled World Wars I and II for its ferocity, for the broad coalitions of support that were engaged by both sides, and for the consequences that the outcome had for the future trajectory of global politics. If the Cold War could in fact be considered World War III, then the Global Jihadi War was World War IV.

Like the Cold War, the Jihadi War was different from World Wars I and II in several significant ways. Unlike the earlier world wars, the Cold War lacked a single military conflagration similar to the European or Pacific theaters. Instead it consisted of a series of smaller fires—such as Korea, Cuba, the Hungarian Uprising, and Vietnam. The coalitions on either side of the Cold War were not as tightly defined as they were in the earlier wars. The notion of the enemy shifted. It was sometimes thought to be an international conspiracy, sometimes a specific power, and at other times a shadowy force that created an internal ideological threat as well as an external military opposition.

In all of these respects, the Global Jihadi War was more like the Cold War than World Wars I and II. In a book that I wrote early in the 1990s, I suggested that the encounter between religious politics and the secular state presented characteristics of global conflict that were similar

---

6. Bacevich, *The New American Militarism*.

to the Cold War.[7] In that book I included a variety of forms of religious activism, including Buddhist militants in Sri Lanka, Sikh and Hindu activists in India, Jewish extremists in Israel, the Christian militia in the United States, as well as Muslim radicals in the Middle East and elsewhere around the world. I continue to hold to this position, that the rise of Islamic political extremism is part of a global phenomenon involving virtually every religious tradition, and that it is related to what I have called the loss of faith in secular nationalism: the erosion of confidence in European and American-style secular democracy to provide a moral base for public order. In an updating of this book published recently, however, I characterized the conflict as a "global rebellion" rather than a new Cold War. But the idea was the same, that the late twentieth century and early twenty first was witness to a global confrontation between secular and religious politics.

The Global Jihadi War represented the most intense and widespread variation of this phenomenon—the West's war with radical Islam. This was the confrontation between the worldwide jihadi movement that focused on the Middle East and the bellicose response that it received from authorities in Europe and the United States. The conflict between secular governments and radical religious movements, including Christian, Jewish, Hindu, and Buddhist ones, can be subsumed under the notion of a new Cold War, but by the twenty-first century that global confrontation was seen primarily as one between Muslim extremism and the politics of the Christian and Jewish West. It was seen as a confrontation between jihadi authoritarianism and democracy, between a radical Islamic communitarianism and a defensive secular individualism buttressed by right-wing Christian and Jewish thought.

Yet the Global Jihadi War was an odd war, in that it was not obviously a struggle over territory. The wars of the twentieth century were in large part about maps—conquering and redefining geographic space. Even the Cold War produced its geographical divisions: North and South Korea, East and West Germany, and North and South Vietnam. The Global Jihadi War was not about land. Although Robert Pape has argued persuasively that most suicide bombers, including those professing a religious ideology, are a part of struggles over contested cultural or territorial space, their wars are defensive rather than aggressive.[8] The

7. Juergensmeyer, *The New Cold War?*
8. Pape, *Dying to Win*.

conflict in its broadest, transnational dimensions is not about the conquest of land but about cultural and political domination.

Groups sharing an al Qaeda perspective may have attacked the very centers of Western power in New York, Madrid, and London, but no one expected an invasion an invasion and occupation of America and European countries to follow. After the collapse of the World Trade Center towers on September 11, few Americans feared that the next move would be an army of jihadi occupation forces breaching Maryland's shores, fighting their way from one suburban mall to another on their way to conquering the American capital. It was not that kind of war. The jihadi threat was not confined to borders. Terrorist attacks could be staged anywhere. The American and European response to the jihadi threat was similarly not a war aimed solely at geographical conquest. Even though the U.S. invaded Afghanistan and Iraq and its armies continued for years to be occupying forces in those countries, no one would seriously have described these as attempts at colonization. Few if any observers even in the Muslim world thought that the United States wanted to annex these two underdeveloped and unhappy nations under its direct political control.

Instead, the Jihadi War, like the Cold War, was in part about political control, but even more significantly about ideas. In saying this I do not mean to belittle the importance of the struggle, for ideas can have enormous power. But because the contest was between differing ways of perceiving the world and the relationship between political and moral order, the struggle had a remarkably moralistic tone. The enemies were not really individuals as much as they were ways of thinking. This means that the enemies, in a personal sense, were largely imagined.

IMAGINED ENEMIES

More than the Cold War, the Global Jihadi War existed largely in the imaginations of both sides of the conflict. All wars are imaginary to some extent, in that the idea of an absolute enemy is something that does not come easily. It is a way of characterizing the source of actions so incomprehensible, so impossible to understand in terms of rational civil behavior, that they are attributed to an absolute evil.

The idea of an enemy is an attempt to make sense of a difficult experience. We like to think that evil things are done by evil people. This idea persists even though we know, as Hannah Arendt said about Nazis involved in the Jewish holocaust in World War II, that there is a "banality" about many evil acts.[9] Horrible things are done by ordinary people in the name of public order or racial superiority or national identity. Often such acts are done in the context of war. What makes the acts evil, and the ones who commit them evildoers, is the way that they are perceived. Hence the idea of enemy—an absolute, intractable, nonnegotiable, and totally evil enemy—is a socially constructed category.

In the Global Jihadi War, the evil enemy is sometimes difficult to discern. In Iraq, for instance, the U.S. presence was intended to be a liberating force. When the Americans arrived in 2003, a Muslim cleric from the Fallujah area told me, initially the military was not regarded as evil. There was a "wait and see" attitude towards the U.S. invasion and occupation of the country.[10] Later, when bungling U.S. military operations were perceived by the local residents as assaults on Iraqi people and Islamic culture, the resistance to U.S. presence hardened into an attitude of war. This in turn created something of a conceptual dilemma for the occupying American troops, who originally had seen the resistance fighters simply as disgruntled locals and old Saddam supporters who did not take kindly to the new regime. But eventually they were seen in the way that all enemies are seen in war—as evil incarnate. On the evening before his battalion was to attack the city of Fallujah, a U.S. marine commander assured his soldiers that they were not going to fight "a faceless enemy." The enemy had a face, he told them: "he's called satan."[11]

The marine commander was simply echoing the words of his Commander-in-Chief George W. Bush who reminded the American people that the resistance struggle in Iraq was supported by "evil people." After the London subway attacks in July 2005, Prime Minister Tony Blair said that the British government was not confronting ordinary criminals or political adversaries in hunting those who helped to perpetrate the crime. Rather, the British government was confronting an "evil ideology."[12]

Anyone who experienced the agony of losing a relative or friend in the vicious car bomb attacks on the streets of Baghdad, the suicide explosions in the London subway, the bomb blasts in Mumbai, or the

9. Arendt, *Eichmann in Jerusalem.*

10. Interview with al-Kubaisi.

11. Quoted by BBC News, November 23, 2004.

12. Quoted by CNN and BBC News, July 19, 2005.

spectacular assault on the World Trade Center, would doubtless agree. Any act of violence, especially one that destroys with the shocking horror of a terrorist attack, is a devastating experience. It is an act of evil as far as the victims and their loved ones are concerned. Most of us would concur: violence is an evil thing.

Yet, for those of us who are trying to make sense out of such acts, it is not enough to stop there. We cannot say simply that evil acts are done by evil people, and pretend that we have understood the situation. This is especially the case when those who have carried out such acts of evil are themselves convinced that they were acting for the moral good. In most cases of violent public acts, the perpetrators regard themselves as responding in kind. They think that they and their people have been violated in an evil way that is commensurate with the acts that they themselves are perpetrating. Hence in a case such as the September 11 attack on the World Trade Center and Pentagon, it appears that a double construction of enemies has taken place. First the jihadi activists construct an image of the U.S. and European powers as an enemy, one that they target for terrorist attacks. Then these attacks cause Americans and Europeans to construct their own image of the jihadis as enemies, one to which they respond with force as well. Finally the jihadis retaliate in their own violent ways, the government authorities in theirs, and thus the war goes on.

In the case of the Global Jihadi War, we might look at this litany of violence and counter-violence and conclude that they started it. The U.S., we might argue, was never really the enemy that they thought it was. Yet even if this assessment is correct, it is something of an academic point. It does not make much difference in the middle of battle who started the fight. After all, from a radical Islamic political perspective, Western powers started the conflict and the jihadi analysis is correct: the historical role of Europe and the U.S. in intruding in the politics and culture of the Middle East created a situation of political oppression to which Muslim activists were responding in kind. But even if one disagrees, and thinks that the European and U.S. influence in the Middle East was essentially benign, or at least not demonic, the fact that the West has been perceived as an aggressive colonial power is itself a reality. This perception can be a powerful motivating force. And it is only a step away from there to seeing the West as an evil force.

In most cases the idea of an evil enemy is a way of imagining who might have done a terrible thing—be it years of dominating a people in a colonial oppression or conducting a terrorist attack on a major city. In most cases these grievances are real. In others, however, the enemy can be imagined with very little justification at all. In the case of the Japanese movement, the Aum Shinrikyo, for example, the imagined enemies were a paranoid cornucopia of political powers and social groups, from the Japanese government and the U.S. military to the Freemasons. When members of the Aum movement unleashed nerve gas in the Japanese subways, however, this fantasy turned into deadly reality.

Images of fantastic war are rife in all aspects of culture, from movies to computer games. They also exist in the enduring images of religion. The literature of virtually all religious traditions are filled with warfare—whether it is the great conflict of the Hindu epics, the Ramayana and Mahabharata; the wars between Buddhist and Tamil kings in the Sri Lankan Chronicles; the great adventures of Japanese and Chinese warriors; the biblical images of warfare in the books of Exodus, Numbers, Deuteronomy, and 1 Samuel; and the great wars of Islamic tradition that can be traced back to the military force of the Prophet. In the case of Christianity it is the ultimate war before the last judgment. In fact, no war could be more cataclysmic than the images of the final confrontation between good and evil that is portrayed in the New Testament book of Revelation.

It is these larger-than-life images of global catastrophe that seized the imagination of many conservative Christians in the United States. The cataclysm described in Revelation 16 is in part a "battle," but it also involves a series of acts of nature presumably triggered by God: "flashes of lightning, rumblings, peals of thunder, and a violent earthquake, such as had not occurred since people were upon the earth" (Rev 16:18). Islands would vanish and mountains would be leveled (Rev 16:20). At the culmination of the conflict the old world would be swept away and "a new heaven and a new earth" would be established (Rev 21:1). A new holy city, a new Jerusalem would be established and God would dwell with the citizens. "See," the book says, "I am making all things new" (Rev 21:5). Some Christian activists see the current Global Jihadi War as that apocalyptic moment described in the book of Revelation. It is sacred war, God's war, once described in the Bible. It is a war that will ultimately lead to spiritual transformation and peace.

Some Islamic activists also saw their struggle as dictated by scripture, but in their case the scripture is the Qur'an. The ninth section of the Qur'an urges the faithful to stand up in righteous defense against "people who have violated their oaths and intended to expel the Messenger" and those who "attack you first" (Surah 9:13). Though the historical context is one in which a fledgling Muslim community is attempting to survive in a hostile environment in the seventh century CE, some Muslims take this passage from the Qur'an as license to struggle against those in the present day who would try to destroy them and their religion. Like the battles in the Christians' New Testament and the Hebrew Bible, it is ultimately not a human battle, but God's war: "fight against them so that Allah will punish them by your hands and disgrace them and give you victory over them and heal the breasts of a believing people" (Surah 9:14).

These ideas of spiritual battle that are found in scripture and employed by activists in such disparate movements as the Aum Shinrikyo, the Christian right and militant Islam, are shadows of an image that rebounds within the worldviews of all religious traditions: the notion of cosmic war. The idea of cosmic war is that of a grand encounter between the forces of good and evil, religion and irreligion, order and chaos, and it is played out on an epic scale. Real-world social and political confrontations can be swept up into this grand scenario. Conflicts over territory and political control are lifted into the high proscenium of sacred drama. Such extraordinary images of cosmic war are meta-justifications for religious violence. They not only explain why religious violence happens—why religious persons feel victimized by violence and why they need to take revenge for this violence—but they also provide a large worldview, a template of meaning in which religious violence makes sense. In the context of cosmic war, righteous people are impressed into service as soldiers and great confrontations occur in which noncombatants are killed. But ultimately the righteous will prevail, for cosmic war is, after all, God's war. And God cannot lose.

The image of cosmic war is often in the background in thinking about war, but worldly war and cosmic war, are not quite the same thing. By "war"—worldly war—I mean the moral absolutism of conflict. It is a way of thinking about a struggle between enemies who cannot be reconciled. War involves imagining enemies who are absolute in two ways: they are a threat to one's very existence, and they are so morally bankrupt that their humanity cannot be redeemed. Hence they *must* be destroyed because they are threatening, and they *can* be destroyed because they are evil. War is a way of seeing the world in which enemies contest with one another in do-or-die combat, in confrontations that are often though not necessarily violent. The potential for violence always lurks within war, however, since one is confronting an evil enemy that if not defused or destroyed will try to destroy the other side.

A "cosmic war" takes this enduring idea of warfare and sees it as sacred struggle—the battle between good and evil, right and wrong, religion and irreligion. It implants these transcendent spiritual mages onto the contemporary social scene. In other words, it magnifies a conflict into God's war. There is nothing specifically Christian or Islamic about this idea of cosmic war. Every religious tradition contains images of moral battles that have a divine valence to them. Hence every religion has a grand martial scenario that can be transported into contemporary conflict and elevate a social or political confrontation into cosmic war.

If war absolutizes conflict, one might well ask whether all wars are to some extent cosmic wars. I think the answer is, in part, yes. Since all wars involve moral absolutism—the idea that enemies are evil—religion is often in the background. Sacred language and images become fused with ideas about warfare. Most wars are thought to be conducted for a high moral purpose, and often this means seeing them as blessed by God. For this reason there is something of a sliding scale between worldly war and cosmic war, between military activities that are rational calculations for the sake of civil order and those that are thought to be manifestations of an ultimate sacred struggle. For the sake of understanding the nature of war, however, it is useful to keep this analytic distinction.

This distinction between worldly war and cosmic war is particularly important in looking back at the Global Jihadi War and making sense of it. On both sides some of the activists took what might appear to be a justifiable position of force and magnified it into a moral struggle of such religious proportions that it became a sacred struggle. The enemies became cosmic foes. This is a danger that exists whenever a conflict is put into the context of war and enemies are defined in absolute terms. In the Global Jihadi War this led to the ability to destroy large numbers of innocent people with moral indifference—or worse, with the joy of thinking that in doing the killing God was on one's side.

WHEN WAR MAKES SENSE

What circumstance could possibly make such thinking about war make sense? The Global Jihadi War is an interesting example. It is almost a textbook case of how war involves imagined enemies. For over a decade in the 1990s and the beginning of the twenty-first century, jihadi activists attacked U.S. military installations, government buildings, and even—in 1993—the World Trade Center. In their minds the jihadi activists imagined themselves to be at war with the United States. During all these years, most Americans thought that the idea that they were seen as enemies was such an inconceivable fantasy that they refused to give it credibility. When one of the jihadi acts of terrorism was spectacularly successful—on September 11, 2001—most Americans were taken by surprise. Despite years of provocation most Americans could not imagine that they were targets of war. "Why do they hate us?" an anguished public asked. In most cases without waiting for an answer or even finding out who the "they" were who hated the United States, many American began to think in these anti-Americans' militant terms. From that moment on many began to adopt the jihadi view of the world, a world at war.

It was a great moment of victory for activists like Khalid Sheikh Mohammad and Osama bin Laden—and not just because of the destruction of the World Trade Center towers and the damage to the Pentagon. The attack itself was successful in that it gave credibility to his rhetoric within the Muslim world. It showed that the warfare about which the jihadis spoke was real, and that the great enemy was vulnerable. Since the jihadi voice was that of an isolated tiny minority among Muslims, these signs of symbolic power were enormously helpful for the jihadi propaganda among potential Muslim supporters.

But even more important from the jihadi activists' point of view, was the fact that the event caused American leaders to adopt the jihadi global war terminology. Any potential Muslim supporter who might have been wavering in deciding whether to give the jihadi message credibility were impressed that America itself began to validate the jihadi view of the world. Moreover, the U.S. response gave Osama bin Laden a sort of backhanded personal honor. He was dubbed as America's great enemy.

At this point, then, the die was cast for war. From the moment that the U.S. military began attacking Afghanistan on October 7, 2001, there was no easy retreat. Once the President of the United States had proclaimed a "war on terrorism," and it was clear that this phrase was not a metaphor—as the Afghan attack amply demonstrated—the war was on. Once the idea of war took hold in the public imagination it was easy to expand its purview to other parts of the world and to incorporate other imagined enemies into its fold. The war in Iraq became a logical extension of the Global Jihadi War. Once war has been proclaimed, and even more important, once it has descended into the thinking of millions on both sides of the conflict, the image of war is not easily dispelled. This is especially so when the casualties on both sides begin to mount. No leader on either side would want to call off war too quickly and risk the appearance that the lives of those soldiers and civilians caught in its crossfire were in vain. By the middle of the first decade of the twenty-first century, the Global Jihadi War was well underway.

In the post-Bush era of American politics the perspective changed and the illusion of warfare began to fade from the scene. But the effects of the thinking about global war will likely resonate for years. Since the idea of cosmic war is largely in the imagination it can dissolve as surely as it appeared. The Global Jihadi War can fade into history as quickly as the Cold War thinking disintegrated after the fall of the Berlin Wall. Yet the possibilities of cosmic conflict endure, where religious imagination can fuel political paranoia and erupt into global war. The conditions persist, alas, for discontent to crystallize into war, and war to descend into cosmic conflict.

BIBLIOGRAPHY

Literature

Arendt, Hannah. *Eichmann in Jerusalem: A Report on the Banality of Evil.* Harmondsworth: Penguin, 1994.

Bacevich, Andrew J. *The New American Militarism.* New York: Oxford University Press, 2005.

Bin Laden, Osama. "Declaration of War Against the Americans Occupying the Lands of the Two Holy Places." *Al Quds Al Arabi* [newspaper]. London, 1996.

Huntington, Samuel P. "The Clash of Civilizations?" *Foreign Affairs* 72/3 (Summer 1993) 22–49.

Juergensmeyer, Mark. *The New Cold War? Religious Nationalism Confronts the Secular State.* Berkeley: University of California Press, 1995; revised version published as *Global Rebellion: Religious Challenges to the Secular State.* Berkeley: University of California Press, 2008.

Pape, Robert. *Dying to Win: The Strategic Logic of Suicide Terrorism.* New York: Random House, 2005.

Interviews

Sheik Muhammad al-Kubaisi, Deputy Secretary General of the Council of Islamic Clergy, Baghdad, Iraq, July 5, 2004.

Mahmud Abouhalima, convicted co-conspirator in the 1993 World Trade Center bombing attack, Lompoc, California, August 19, 1997.

3

Apocalyptic Speculations and the War of Armageddon

GÖRAN GUNNER

The phenomenon of *Left Behind* is now well established as a series of books, novels, and films. It deals with end-time theology and, thus, the end of this world. Different aspects of *Left Behind* have subsequently been dealt with in a lot of books and articles.[1] In this chapter I will concentrate on recent developments but against the background of what has been labelled Armageddon-theology. I will use the *Left Behind* concept in the shape of a computer game as an example. In this game, there is a theological assumption expecting a violent end of the world through major upcoming war/wars. The *Left Behind* computer game, as well as the Armageddon-theology, is about the end of the time and anticipates an extremely violent ending, with a world war and bloodshed. The motivation for Armageddon-theology and the *Left Behind* concept as a whole is taken from a specific Christian interpretation of the Bible usually named dispensationalism.

Through the novels in the *Left Behind* series the reader gets involved by reading and imagining but with the computer game *Left Behind* the player is involved in taking active measures on the right side while fighting the evil forces. The player is in need of taking decisions, including

---

1. See for example: Gunner, "9/11 and Armageddon"; Rossing, *The Rapture Exposed*; Frykholm, *Rapture Culture*; and Shuck, *Marks of the Beast*.

the use of military weapons in the fight against the enemies of God. You do no longer need to wait for God to orchestrate his master plan but you can do it with the help of the end-time forces in the name of God.

FICTION AND THE BIBLE

The *Left Behind* series is undoubtedly in the genre of fiction. At the well-known bookseller Barnes & Nobles, its books are placed in a bookshelf named as "Religious Fiction." The categorization seems very well to pin-point the basic intention behind the books—to produce religious truth in the form of fiction. For people identifying with the dispensationalist ideas, the truth, as considered to be the biblical faith, is important. There is always only one truth and that is the word of God literally written in the Scripture. Two ways are possible for the individual—you either say "yes" or you say "no"—you are "Bible-believing" or you are not.

Thus, religious fiction seems to construct an "unholy" alliance between fiction and reality and even with what is considered to be the truth. Used in Evangelical prophesy, concepts like Rapture,[2] tribulation,[3] Antichrist,[4] Armageddon,[5] and the end-time war, seem to become an important instrument for letting fantasy, the Scripture, and present-day events in the world join hands. The world events of today involve unpredicted catastrophes as well as actions taken by the worldly powers but at the same time each individual is in need of salvation and to ensure being part of the saved entity, ready to meet with Jesus in the Rapture.

The fiction is nurtured by the Bible where everything is believed to fit into the plan of God and fuelled by a careful reading of newspapers and watching television newscast. Fantasy, Bible, and politics make up a delicate mixture and become the guide. Through this combination, fiction becomes a confirmation of the truth.

---

2. The rapture is in dispensational theology the future event when Jesus is expected to descend from heaven to meet in the sky with the uplifted true Christians, named as the Bride.

3. The tribulation is the period following the Rapture. On earth there will appear seven years of tribulation.

4. Antichrist is considered to have the world-power during the tribulation.

5. The tribulation is ending with the battle of Armageddon. The battle ends with the second coming of Christ destroying all the world armies who are attacking the State of Israel.

Amy Johnson Frykholm interprets *Left Behind* as belonging both to the fundamentalist tradition[6] with specific reference to the dispensationalist history and to American popular apocalyptic culture.[7] She has made interviews with persons living in the context of the *Left Behind* belief, and she draws conclusions about the readers being between fiction and truth:

> Yes, the books are accurate according to what they know of the Bible, but, as many readers remind me, this is "only" fiction, "just one person's interpretation" . . . At the same time, the lightness with which readers accept the books, the lack of authority the novels have because of their status as fiction, paradoxically opens the door wider for the books' ideological work. Readers . . . can read for fun, for pleasure, getting caught up in characters' lives and the presentation of images. When they return to the biblical text, these images, received through the innocuous means of entertainment, give shape and meaning to the previously obscure text, making it come alive in a way it previously had not. This lends an authority to *Left Behind* that often goes unacknowledged by readers.[8]

Amy Johnson Frykholm reveals a pattern where the readers of *Left Behind* declare the book to be "only fiction" but at the same time they give it divine authority concerning the coming judgement of God. This gives the reader "the power to 'see' its truth and experience it in a way that is almost visceral."[9] So it seems that the series of books and films belonging to the *Left Behind* create a very important sense of belonging, of being saved, of being on the right side, and in control of what is going on in the world. The events happening in the world as well as the readers, are included in the plan of God. In this way everything makes sense, as explained by Rossing:

> The genius of the *Left Behind* novels is their use of fiction to advance a political and theological agenda. *Left Behind* creates a comprehensive, compelling fictitious world of people—people "just like you and me" (. . .) *Left Behind* gets inside people's

---

6. For more about definitions, see below.
7. Frykholm, *Rapture Culture*, 13–14.
8. Ibid., 133.
9. Ibid., 138.

heads to try to convince us that the violent, absolutist script is how God's victory will happen and is happening in the world.[10]

A GAME—BUT ACCORDING TO THE BIBLE?

The *Left Behind* series written by Tim LaHaye and Jerry B. Jenkins consists today of at least fifteen basic volumes[11] but includes also a special Kids Series, a Military Series,[12] a Political Series,[13] and what is named Non-Fiction.[14] But the *Left Behind* concept has also been transformed into a CD with *Left Behind Worship*, films and videos, and computer games as *Left Behind: Eternal Forces* and *Left Behind: Tribulation Forces*.

It is worth mentioning that one of the authors, Tim LaHaye, was pastor in a San Diego church for twenty-five years. He has been active for conservative values as well as in political activism, not the least in support of the Republican party in different elections including support for Mike Huckabee for presidency in 2008.

Compared with other computer games, the *Left Behind* games may appear as a peaceful alternative. Still, there is a question about what happens if there are aspirations of being fiction but at the same time of introducing the truth. In the introduction to the game it is for sure stated that the story is a fictional novel but in the next sentence it is declared that the novel is based on "prophecies from the Bible's Book of Revelation." Continuing with explaining different concepts, these are said to be according to Scripture.

The concept "Christianity" does not appear in either the game or in the game manual but "believers" and "nonbelievers" are used. Of course, that is due to the point of departure in the *Left Behind* starting with the Rapture and the events closely following. In the dispensational theology as well as in the game, that is where the Christians already through the Rapture are taken away. The people left to struggle on earth are those left behind and coming to believe after what they have seen happening or

10. Rossing, *The Rapture Exposed*, xi.

11. With titles as *Tribulation Force*; *The Mark*; and *Armageddon*.

12. With titles as *Apocalypse Dawn*; *Apocalypse Crucible*; and *Apocalypse Burning*.

13. With titles as *End of State*; *Impeachable Offense*; and *Necessary Evils*.

14. With at least twelve books, including *Are We Living in the End Times?*; *Perhaps Today*; and *The Promise of Heaven*.

still continuing as nonbelievers. The manual to the game states that this is according to the Bible:

> According to Biblical Scripture, when the Rapture comes the Lord will take His people to Heaven leaving others "left behind" on Earth to face the emerging antichrist.[15]

However, coming up in the levels of the game you are immediately introduced to Christian concepts as disciples, evangelists, and missionaries. The Tribulation Force acting in the city of New York are the good guys while the Global Community Peacekeepers force—the Antichrist's forces—as such are the bad guys. Playing the game you can visit the "house of wisdom" and get answers concerning food, money, and spirituality. When visiting "Scripture" you will find a scroll providing you with the word of God. The heading of "Lessons" gives teaching about, for example, creationism, archaeology, prophetic messages, and theology. The ambition of the creators of the game is clearly to strengthen the believers and to involve nonbelievers in Christianity when playing the game:

> You will soon be immersed in an apocalyptic world delivering a positive moral message . . . For those who are not believers of any faith, this game will not only entertain you with great game play, you will be encouraged to think about matters of eternal importance . . .[16]

> Join the ultimate fight of Good versus Evil, commanding Tribulation Forces, the Global Community Peacekeepers![17]

In the online information about the game, the Tribulation Force is also identified as "the all new American Militia." The mission is to recruit new members and to get your force growing and thereby saving as many as possible from the clutches of Antichrist.

> Spiritual warfare is the crux of the time remaining before Armageddon. A spiritual battle is gearing up throughout the streets of New York City, and around the entire globe. Truly, we are not battling flesh and blood, but against unseen principalities and powers. As we get closer to the Battle of Armageddon, spiritual warfare is the most important weapon we have against the enemy. Nonviolent, and only seeking to expose the truth—

15. *Left Behind: Eternal Forces*, 9–10.
16. Ibid., 2.
17. *Left Behind: Tribulation*.

the influencers of the Tribulation Force are at the forefront of bringing a message of hope to a world being deceived by the antichrist.[18]

This spiritual warfare is not enough. Besides prayer warriors and worship leaders there is a need for more action to be taken by the player: "Control more than 40 units types—from Prayer Warrior and Worship Leaders to Spies, Special Forces and Battle Tanks!"[19]

In the game, there are possibilities for you as a player to take action in physical warfare through establishing a force of soldiers. At each level the abilities, beside prayer and spiritual warfare, are increasing. At level one, the soldiers, the good guys, are always at the frontline but not allowed to shoot unless being attacked. On the second level the soldiers can sacrifice the defensive capabilities and instead get explosive bullets and thus become more deadly. These soldiers may also be part of an elite force while being trained as a spy or a sniper.

The soldier at the next level is more skilfully trained and "more deadly" with the possibility to use explosive bullets. The soldiers at the third level are trained at the Mission Training Center:

> These are the best trained combatants in the world, capable of intense fighting—on the front line, or deep inside enemy dominated areas. Capable of moving invisibly for short periods of time, and able to utilize Silent Attack techniques when so ordered—the Elite Force team-member is the ultimate physical warrior in Eternal Forces.[20]

But building up an army with soldiers is not enough. To be successful in fighting, the player also needs military vehicles and powerful weapons. The player may use static defence as an armed and armoured turret. Other alternatives are Humvee vehicles that are armed with .50 calibre machine guns, the United States Army Abrams tanks, and helicopters for light combat operations.

> In the final years preceding Armageddon, you will be forced to act to defend your people from hostile lethal forces. There is no holding back. The Global Community does not want us to be

18. *Left Behind: Eternal Forces*, 30.

19. Left Behind Games, INC., 2007. Online: http://www.leftbehindgames.com/pages/the_games.htm. A fourth version of the program was introduced in 2011. Online: http://www.leftbehindgames.com/LBGames2011Catalog.pdf.

20. *Left Behind: Eternal Forces*, 34.

successful in our outreach. And without Soldiers, you will be completely unprepared for armed combat. Soldiers have made themselves available to defend your forces from bodily harm and death. However, you must remember that your Soldiers are on the front lines for TWO battles—the spiritual warfare is just as real as the physical warfare, especially for them.[21]

The *Left Behind* games are produced in the setting of an unavoidable upcoming war. There is not anything unusual with that, since the Armageddon-literature is expecting tribulation and war in the end-time. But the ordinary way of putting it is that everything is according to the plan of God and in the hands of God. The moral message in the *Left Behind* games seems to be that according to the word of God you may use not only prayer but physical warfare if needed. You as an individual may take action on behalf of God. If it is considered that according to the Scriptures, an individual can use weapons in war during the time of tribulation, the conclusion can be that you may give God a helping hand through warfare in other situations. Usually, peace-keeping forces are connected with for instance the United Nations and considered to perform a desirable duty. In the *Left Behind* concept the peace-keeping forces are the evil ones. This seems to foster the idea that according to the Bible the peace-keeping forces are a legitimate target to be fought in a war.

It is possible to conclude that the *Left Behind* fosters a readiness for a political activism on behalf of God, including a motivation for Christians to join for spiritual values and political action. But this is not enough. *Left Behind* argues for a need of being prepared to take military action. This is something not just for states and worldly powers. As a Bible-believing individual it may be your duty to be a soldier with arms in your hands and if needed to be ready to kill the enemies of God.

SOME MORE ABOUT DEFINITIONS

Whatever categorization we use for labelling the *Left Behind*, it is not satisfactory or all-inclusive. That goes also for fundamentalism, Dispensationalism, evangelical, Christian Zionist, Christian right, or Armageddon-theology, for example. Behind ideas such as *Left Behind* there are a variety of interpretations and a diversity of denominations,

21. Ibid., 33.

congregations, groups, and individuals. To use an evangelical example, we will find on one side those evangelicals preaching the gospel of prosperity and on the other side left-wing evangelicals critical to prosperity, such as the *Sojourners*. We will find evangelicals all the way from those naming themselves Christians Zionists, as the International Christian Embassy in Jerusalem, to groups like Evangelicals for Middle-Eastern understanding.

The Christian right is by Mark Taylor defined as conservative Protestants that "adhere to and [are] committed to developing an aggressive American political romanticism."[22] Barbara Rossing names this theology, expecting millions of people to be killed and Jesus to be a warrior killing those disagreeing with him, a theology similar to "Dominionism" or "Christian Recontructionism."[23] Chris Hedges talks about a tiny minority named as radical fundamentalist and Christian Dominionists. They have the intention to take over the machinery of U.S. state and religious institutions.[24] Stephen Sizer, in his book about Christian Zionism, talks about the popular literature coming out of the U.S. as apocalyptic dispensational pro-Zionism.[25] Timothy Weber is using the concepts evangelical and mainly dispensational concerning the ideas of interest in this chapter.[26] Finally, Grace Halsell used, already in the middle of the 1980s, the concept Armageddon-theology and concluded that the message derived from the Armageddon-theology was evident: since "war is inevitable, so let's get on with it."[27]

DISPENSATIONALISM AND THE NUCLEAR ARMAGEDDON

One of the main roots of the contemporary *Left Behind* theology is to be found in the so-called dispensationalism of the nineteenth century. dispensational theology develops a methodology to interpret the biblical prophesies as being fulfilled in actual contemporary events. Through the prophesy interpretation, the dispensationalists look upon the course of history as consisting of a number of dispensations, sequential periods.

22. Taylor, *Religion, Politics*, x.

23. Rossing, *The Rapture Exposed*, ix.

24. Hedges, *American Fascist*, 19.

25. For the history of Christian Zionism, see for example Gunner, *När tiden tar slut*; Sizer, *Christian Zionism*; Clark, *Allies for Armageddon*.

26. Weber, *On the Road*.

27. Halsell, *Prophecy and Politics*, 10.

The focus is put on the periods that include the end of this world and the upcoming final battle between God and Satan, culminating in the furious battle of Armageddon.

It is not easy to calculate the impact of this kind of theology but for sure, there is a huge group of followers in United States as well as smaller pockets of supporters in other countries in the Western world. The *Left Behind* series is calculated to have been sold in 60 million copies. A predecessor in the 1970s, in the category of "non-fiction," was *The Late Great Planet Earth* by Hal Lindsey, which sold more than 40 million copies. Lindsey was followed by several televangelists, such as Jerry Falwell, Pat Robertson, Jimmy Swaggart, and John Hagee. Millions of U.S. citizens followed the message concerning a flourishing and territorially expanding Israel, and the coming catastrophes. At the same time, born-again Christians were promised salvation with the second coming of Christ and escape from the tribulation to come.

Hal Lindsey, at the time, popularized dispensational theology and for more than forty years he continued to publish books and DVDs. As an example, he has published DVDs, videos, and books with titles like: *The Road to Holocaust* (1989), *Middle East Ready for War* (2002), *The Oslo Accords: A Decade of Deception and Failure* (2004), and *The Everlasting Hatred: The Roots of Jihad* (2011). In these productions there is no intention at all of doing fiction—it is the truth, the Bible-believing way of looking upon the world and what is going to happen in the near future. Reading his books easily show that the interpretation changes by time even if he is using the same biblical quotations and is always expecting the war to appear.

In his "Armageddon theology" Hal Lindsey assumes that during the Cold War period the Soviet Union was the big enemy.[28] A Communist assault led by Russia would, according to Lindsey, be directed against Jerusalem and Israel. In 1982 he published the book *The 1980's: Countdown to Armageddon*. Lindsey interprets Romans 13 and finds several important principles:

> God ordained governments to keep order and peace, and provide protection for their citizens and their property;
>
> - God ordained an officer with a sword to enforce the law to protect the innocent and punish the guilty;

28. See Gunner, "9/11 and Armageddon."

- Whatever nation attacks the life, liberty and property of others, its government or leaders must be punished.[29]

Lindsey concludes that the Bible supports the building up of a powerful military force and that the U.S. would assume that role. This is of major significance since a weak U.S., according to Lindsey, would encourage the Soviet Union to start an all-out war (which Lindsey also predicted).

> We need to elect men and women who will have the courage to make the tough decisions needed to insure our nation's survival. They must be willing to clamp down on big government, cut exploitation of the welfare system, keep our strong commitments to our allies and stand up to communist expansion. We need people who see how important a strong military is to keeping peace for us and what remains of the free world.[30]

We can talk about a rather typical dispensationalist paradox, namely that U.S. should be ready to fight for "peace and freedom," ready to use all its available military might, while, at the same time, assuming that the final destruction is unavoidable. There is a readiness in the dispensationalist "Armageddon theology" for ordinary men and women—at least at top positions in the society—to be ready to act. The final war in the shape of Armageddon is closer than ever, and it seems that human beings are prepared to spark off the battle on behalf of God. And this is not just part of the "ordinary struggle" in the world but considered to be according to the Bible and included in the divine plan of God.

Armageddon-theology in general puts the hope in Christians in situations of power and then mainly belonging to the U.S. administration. If we compare with *Left Behind* it is possible to conclude *Left Behind* seems to involve every Christian individual as a potential soldier in the militant struggle on God's side.

THE OLD AND NEW ENEMY—
ANTICHRIST, ISLAM, AND TERROR

The final battle of Armageddon in dispensational theology is geographically placed in the State of Israel and it is the forces of Antichrist attacking the Jewish state. Even if everything is considered to follow the plan of

29. Lindsey, *The 1980's*, 148.
30. Ibid., 157.

God, a main interest in Armageddon-theology has been to identify both Antichrist and his enemy forces.

In the 1960s and 1970s the Soviet Union was on the agenda with the assumed threat of Communism and the coming Russian invasion of Israel. On the book covers of dispensational books we can, as an example, see the Soviet tanks entering Israel. In the 1980s the focus is on an assumed coming evil ruler of Islam pictured as the Ayatollah Khomeini in Iran or the president Saddam Hussein in Iraq.

Even the tragic events of 9/11 had to be understood as being part of the plan of God in terms of an apocalyptic interpretations and speculations, according to this view. In the Armageddon-theology circles in U.S., it became necessary after 9/11 to situate U.S. in the God-ordained schedule for the end of the world. Thus, several publications by well-established authors were published, and which incorporate America/U.S. in the book title, such as *Attack on America: New York, Jerusalem, and the Role of Terrorism in the Last Days*; *Terror Over America: Understanding the Tragedy*; *Unholy War: America, Israel and Radical Islam*; and *Is America in Bible Prophecy?* In the time before the Rapture, it is self-evident to the Armageddon-theology authors to look upon U.S. as the leading nation of the entire world. The arguments are the following:

God has a plan, and is in control of whatever happens:

- The U.S. is the most powerful nation in the history of the world, and the only superpower in the world today

- The U.S. represents global democracy, Western values such as freedom of religion and choice and respect for human rights.

To be the world-leading nation is also something worth defending according to this view. A threat, and especially a threat against the State of Israel and the Jewish people, should be removed and completely destroyed. All in the name of God.

In the Armageddon-theology of today, the future of the Middle East is connected with concepts as "War" and "Terror." In this kind of interpretation there is no place for negotiations between Israelis and Palestinians and no place for peace. Instead there is an expectation on a coming major catastrophe in the Middle East. The end-time scenario is showing up very soon. Islam will, according to the Armageddon-theology, play a decisive role. In the iconography on book covers, war takes a prominent position with soldiers, tanks, and warplanes. But the intention is to provide evidence that God is in control and is actually directing the force of history even when the military powers of states are included.

The language of the Armageddon-theology identifies completely with an unavoidable final war but is, at the same time, asking for support of ongoing wars and concerns of the U.S. The authors express it like:

> We are at war with terrorism;
> Our war against international Islamic terrorism;
> We are now involved in a life and death war against Islamic terrorism;
> We need warriors![31]

In his book following the 9/11, Jeffrey explains:

> We will marshal the military, intelligence, and political forces of the West to utterly destroy those terrorists who have declared war on our freedoms, our right to religious choice, and our modern democratic values.[32]

It seems that the expectation for a war directed by God is mixed up with ongoing U.S. wars on the world arena. On one hand, the Armageddon-theology is eagerly waiting for the end-time and expect it to take place any minute with Islam as an important player. On the other hand, it wants the U.S. to take any possible military action to prevent the enemy forces. The ideology talks about the end-time war but action talks about world politics.

JOHN HAGEE AND THE UPGRADING
OF THE POLITICAL AGENDA

John Hagee is pastor in the megachurch Cornerstone Church in San Antonio, Texas. He is a well-known TV evangelist and his TV programs are daily on the air through the Global Evangelism Television. He has published plenty of books and the focus in his ministry is on the end-time and the Middle East. This is obvious already through his book titles: *The Beginning of the End: The Assassination of Yitzhak Rabin and the Coming Antichrist* (1996), *Attack on America: New York, Jerusalem, and*

---

31. Price, *Unholy War*, 26; Jeffrey, *War on Terror*, 11, 15; Hagee, *Attack on America*, 5.
32. Jeffrey, *War on Terror*, 15.

the Role of Terrorism in the Last Days (2001), *The Battle for Jerusalem* (2001), *Jerusalem Countdown* (2006), *In Defense of Israel: The Bible's Mandate for Supporting The Jewish State* (2007), *Can America Survive?* (2010), and *Earth's Final Moments* (2011).

The United States and its president are on the wrong way. The policy taken by the U.S. administration is not at all supportive enough to the State of Israel. Since God is blessing those blessing Israel and punishing those not blessing Israel, the U.S. is at risk. In his book following 9/11, Hagee declared the attack took place because U.S. is weak without any will to crush the terrorists.

> Simply stated, America has mocked God! The tragedy of the twin towers in New York is a fiery trial sent to drive us back to the God of Abraham, Isaac, and Jacob. Can America descend any lower into the cesspool of immorality? . . . The tragedy of the twin towers in New York is a fiery trial sent to drive us back to the God of Abraham, Isaac, and Jacob. America has committed every sin of Sodom and Gomorrah, and just as God's judgement came to Sodom and Gomorrah, it is now being poured out upon America.[33]

At the same time, the terrorists should not be unpunished. Hagee puts it this way:

> The question is, do we have the will to stop making excuses and take military action against them and their sponsors? America will either take bold, aggressive action and win, or we will continue to make excuses and lose.[34]

In an interview with Glen Beck at CNN, Hagee reflects on those two slants. It is about the end-time and it is about U.S. military actions. The first quotation is about Antichrist and the second about Iran:

> One, he's going to come as a prince of peace, he's going to establish a one world government, and he's going to establish a one world religion and now there are many religious believers, religious theologians who believe that perhaps that one world religion that he's talking about is Islam because one of the things that happens in the tribulation period, and the tribulation period is the seven-year period that happens on the Earth when there's such devastation that happens on the planet such that anyone

33. Hagee, *Attack on America*, 11.
34. Ibid., 5.

who does not receive the faith of the antichrist is beheaded, and beheading is the methodology of execution of Islam.

I think that the United States should put everything on the table and quit talking about the problem and solve the problem. Everyone says that Iran is killing one third of our people in the field of combat in Iraq. That's an act of war. That gives us the license to go in, to take action without dancing with the United Nations for the rest of our lives, but no one in Washington seems willing to do that. I'll assure you whatever it takes, forces on the ground, a military preemptive strike to destroy his nuclear capacity to produce nuclear weapons. If we don't do it, Israel will have to do it because Israel knows they are number one on his hit list and they have the muscle to back him down.[35]

In order to get U.S. on the right track—morally and militarily—there is a need of lobbying. John Hagee himself is a frequent speaker at conferences organized by Christian Zionists. He is also founder of Christians United for Israel (CUFI) with the aim of doing lobbyism. As an example, the organization has arranged "Nights to Honor Israel" in more than seventy-five major cities across America. CUFI also arranges annual Washington summits.

It is not easy all the time to be sure what are ideas about the end-time and what is political support for the State of Israel. Hagee was, during the 2008 Washington summit, talking about opposition to an Israeli-Palestinian peace, a disparaging of Islam, and focus on hostility to Iran where, according to Hagee, the President is planning for a nuclear holocaust. But all was in the setting of lobbying support for his interpretation of Israel, not the least in the Congress and the Senate. Hagee wants to stress that God is blessing those who support Israel. At the same time God will punish every enemy. In one of his speeches Hagee focused on the enemies of Israel:

Therefore I'm saying today based upon the periodical of God. The nations that come against Israel are in serious trouble. Iran, you are in serious trouble. Damascus you are in serious trouble . . . Russia, you are in serious trouble.[36]

35. "Pastor John Hagee."

36. Extracts from the 2008 Washington summit are online: http://www.jewsonfirst.org/08a/cufi_dc08.html.

It is possible to see a mixture between political lobbyism and prophesy interpretation. In this kind of Armageddon-theology or Christian Zionism, war is what to expect in the near future. These are necessary war(s) to allow the biblical prophesies to be fulfilled and the longed-for end of the world to come. But coming to U.S. politics, this theology urges the incumbent administration to take firm action with military strikes to prevent the worldly enemy from becoming the biblical enemy. Anyhow, in one or another way, what to anticipate for tomorrow is war. But then the true Christians are already taken away in the Rapture and all others are *Left Behind.*

It is possible to conclude that the *Left Behind* fosters a readiness for a political activism on behalf of God, including a motivation for Christians to join for spiritual values and political action. But this is not enough. *Left Behind* argues for a need of being prepared to take military action. This is something not just for states and worldly powers. As a Bible-believing individual, it may be your duty to be a soldier with arms in your hands and, if needed, to be ready to kill the enemies of God.

BIBLIOGRAPHY

Clark, Victoria. *Allies for Armageddon: The Rise of Christian Zionism.* New Haven: Yale University Press, 2007.

Frykholm, Amy Johnson. *Rapture Culture: Left Behind in Evangelical America.* Oxford: Oxford University Press, 2004.

Gunner, Göran. *När tiden tar slut. Motivförskjutningar i frikyrklig apokalyptisk tolkning av det judiska folket och staten Israel.* Studia Theologica Holmiensia 1 and Studia Missionalia Upsaliensia 64. Uppsala: Uppsala Universitet, 1996.

———. "9/11 and Armageddon: The Christian Right and George W. Bush." *Holy Land Studies* 2/1 (September 2003) 33–50.

Hagee, John. *Attack on America: New York, Jerusalem and the Role of Terrorism in the Last Days.* Nashville: Thomas Nelson, 2001.

Halsell, Grace. *Prophecy and Politics: Militant Evangelicals on the Road to Nuclear War.* Westport, CT: Lawrence Hill, 1986.

Hedges, Chris. *American Fascists: The Christian Right and the War on America.* New York: Free Press, 2006.

Jeffrey, Grant R. *War on Terror: Unfolding Bible Prophesy?* Toronto: Frontier Research, 2002.

Left Behind: Eternal Forces: The PC Game: Game Manual. Left Behind Games Inc., 2006.

Left Behind: Tribulation Forces [Chapter 2 of the PC game]. Left Behind Games Inc., 2006. Online: http://www.lbgstore.com/left-behind-eternal-forces-the-pc-game--the-multiplayer-enhancemen.html.

Lindsey, Hal. *The Late Great Planet Earth.* Grand Rapids: Zondervan, 1970.

———. *The 1980's: Countdown to Armageddon.* New York: Bantam, 1982.

"Pastor John Hagee Speaks Out." *Glenn Beck Program*. October 9, 2007. Online: http://archive.glennbeck.com/news/10092007a.shtml.

Price, Randall. *Unholy War: America, Israel, and Radical Islam*. Eugene: Harvest House, 2001.

Rossing, Barbara R. *The Rapture Exposed: The Message of Hope in the Book of Revelation*. New York: Basic Books, 2004.

Shuck, Glenn W. *Mark of the Beast: The Left Behind Novels and the Struggle for Evangelical Identity*. New York: New York University Press, 2005.

Sizer, Stephen. *Christian Zionism: Road-Map to Armageddon?* Leicester: InterVarsity, 2004.

Taylor, Mark Lewis. *Religion, Politics, and the Christian Right: Post-9/11 Powers and American Empire*. Minneapolis: Augsburg Fortress, 2005.

Weber, Timothy P. *On the Road to Armageddon: How Evangelicals Became Israel's Best Friend*. Grand Rapids: Baker, 2004.

4

"It Was the Work of Satan"

Perpetrators Rationalize the Atrocities
of the Rwanda Genocide

ANNE N. KUBAI

From 1994, Rwanda has been characterized in different ways.[1] Some see it as a success story of a country that has been reconstructed from the ashes of genocide, with a growth rate at par with other African countries, building many new roads, schools, and health facilities. More than fifty thousands of ex-combatants have been demobilized and the local and national elections in 2003 were deemed free and fair by many observers.[2] In addition, three and a half million refugees had been repatriated and resettled by 2003[3] and this number has continued to rise since the repatriation is still ongoing.[4] Also, Rwanda stands out as the country with the highest number of women in parliament, which at one point stood at 56 percent.[5] For this achievement the government has earned admiration from several quarters.

1. Uvin, *Aiding Violence.*

2. Samset and Kubai, *Evaluation of Released Prisoners' Project.*

3. See speech by president Kagame at the Commonwealth Club, San Francisco, March 7, 2003, cited in Jha and Yadav, *Rwanda Towards Reconciliation*, 112.

4. Thousands of refugees have been repatriated from Uganda and the process is still going on. At least 20,000 Rwandan refugees are reported to be living is different camps in Uganda (*Staff Reporter*, Kigali, July 11, 2009).

5. According to *Washington Post Foreign Service*, October 27, 2008, Rwanda's parliament "is the first in the world where women claim the majority—56 percent, including the speaker's chair."

Nonetheless others say that:

> Rwanda is still a country ridden with ideology, an ideology communicated from the top—from state—to the people below. The state preaches about good morals, rules and good versus bad habits. People must follow the rules and attend village meetings or they risk being fined. "Solidarity camps" or *ingando* have been set up as rehabilitation for former prisoners on their way back into society as well as retraining for people coming into new administrative positions. Unity and reconciliation are key concepts in the government ideology of today.[6]

In the words of Paul Kagame, the president of Rwanda:

> Genocide is central to the history of Rwanda and Rwandans because it is an expression of what went so badly wrong in our history. We must therefore understand the causes of the problem, confront them and address them. It plays a central role, it tells us about our history, it tells us about the present and it tells us about the future as well, informing us that if we are to move into the future with hope, there are certain issues that we must address without question. Otherwise there is always a danger that if we do things wrong, there is a possibility of sliding back . . . So reason will have to prevail in informing everyone that we cannot have a repeat of this kind of thing at any cost.[7]

In these words, President Kagame spells out the difficult task ahead for his government and the society as a whole—evidently certain things have to be done outright and reason has to prevail in the given circumstances. But it should be born in mind that "the population as a whole is far from ready to establish a collective picture of this historical tragedy."[8]

Seventeen years after the 1994 genocide in Rwanda, its effects are still clearly visible and the process of bringing about reconciliation and at the same time doing justice to thousands of victims and perpetrators poses one of the greatest challenges to its government and the society in general. In the immediate aftermath of the genocide—August/September 1994—about two hundred thousand genocide suspects were held in prisons across the country.[9] It goes without saying that this large

6. Kaplan, *Children in Genocide*, 177.

7. Excerpt of an interview with President Kagame, *The East African Standard*, June 5, 2003, cited in Jha and Yadav, *Rwanda Towards Reconciliation*, 123.

8. Kaplan, *Children in Genocide*, 179.

9. Kubai, "Living in the Shadow of Genocide," 50.

number of prisoners posed serious challenges: detention facilities were overcrowded and it was a strenuous economic burden, not to mention the emotional and financial strain on the families of the detainees, who also had to cope with the stigma of being regarded as *genocidaires*. This called for urgent remedial measures and following the Genocide Statutes of 1996 and provisional releases in 2003, in May 2004, and in July 2005 plus the introduction of the *gacaca* process,[10] the numbers were reduced drastically. By July 2007, it was estimated that only about fifty thousand detainees were incarcerated.[11] On the one hand, the trauma and suffering emanating from the detention of this large number of persons still lingers on, a situation that will continue to have enduring negative impact upon the entire society. On the other hand, the release of large numbers of prisoners accused of genocide crimes, in order for them to participate in the *gacaca* justice process, inevitably became an additional psychological burden for the survivors and victims of the atrocities who often have to live in the same community as their tormenters. This evidently complicates the efforts to bring about peace between the identity groups and harmony for the society in general.

Beneath this is what can be described as fault lines in the post genocide population—there are invisible, but real lines of demarcation which roughly divide the society into three broad categories: the returnees, that is, a large proportion of the population (about four million)[12] that returned from exile often as survivors/victims; those who never left the country during the genocide, mainly Hutu; and finally, the perpetrators or *genocidaires,* i.e., those accused of perpetrating the genocide and today are either in prison or are yet to be brought to justice. Admittedly, finding a balance between justice and reconciliation, or between retribu-

10. Following laid down rules and procedures that were known to the community in the traditional justice system known as *Gacaca*, elders and community leaders would sit on the soft green grass that is found across Rwanda to hear, discuss and resolve conflicts between groups or individuals. With a fair amount of political will, the government reorganized and formalized *Gacaca* and 11,000 *Gacaca courts* were subsequently established throughout the country to try thousands of perpetrators of genocide. For more detailed discussion of the merits and challenges of *Gacaca*, see Kubai, "Between Justice and Reconciliation"; Kubai, "Gacaca and Post-Genocide Reconstruction in Rwanda."

11. In early 2003, the government released close to 25,000 provisionally, many of them having confessed to participating in genocide. Again in 2005 (the third provisional since 2003), 36,000 suspects were released to await the gacaca trials.

12. Jha and Yadav, *Rwanda Towards Reconciliation*, 115.

tion and forgiveness, is a delicate process. President Kagame also admits that "a mix of reconciliation and justice is a challenging balancing act."[13] Perpetrators are also wounded and cannot easily accept guilt and shame for their actions, thus healing and reconciliation become difficult; yet without these, there is a risk of sliding back.

Following the 1994 genocide, the devastation was vast and the shock was enormous for the entire society—perpetrators and survivors alike; and the society is permeated with conflict which can be identified at the following levels:

1. First, the interpersonal level, where individuals may be bitter with others who may have contributed to the death of family or friends. On the one hand, this is complicated by the sense of injustice and loss with which they have to live for rest of their lives. On the other, many perpetrators have to come to terms with a sense of guilt and shame with which they too, have to live for the rest of their lives.

2. Secondly, the intercommunal level, where members of different identity groups are still suspicious of each other. As I have shown elsewhere,[14] this mistrust has manifested itself in what is termed as the genocide ideology which is said to pervade the entire country.[15]

3. Thirdly, is the unwitting outcome of the national peace process that has inevitably exposed both the perpetrators and the victims to public scrutiny, especially during the *Gacaca* trials. Revelations of the chilling details of how the killings of individual persons and families were carried out during the genocide have produced unexpected effects of anger and revenge; and hence fear for both the witnesses and the accused. Also, the requirement that all truth must be told publically has resulted in incriminating others who may not have been identified as perpetrators, thus adding another dimension to the already existing communal tensions.

Many scholars have spent an enormous amount of time and resources debating the causes of the Rwandan genocide and explaining the feroc-

---

13. Jha and Yadav, *Rwanda Towards Reconciliation*, 126.
14. Kubai, "Between Justice and Reconciliation."
15. "Genocide Ideology and the Strategies for Its Eradication."

ity with which it was executed by the ordinary folk. Others have attended to religion and politics in Rwanda,[16] and more recently the focus has shifted to the role of the church in the genocide.[17] The result of this undertaking is a colossal amount of literature, in addition to numerous eyewitness accounts of the killings from the first day that are indelibly imprinted in the memory of many Rwandans who experienced these events only sixteen years ago. However, except for two studies,[18] which present interviews with the perpetrators, many accounts of the Rwanda genocide have omitted the perpetrators' rationalization of the genocide. Also little attention has been given to the use spiritual resources in dealing with the post genocide situation, which is fraught with conflict.

This chapter sets out with two aims: first, to illustrate how the perpetrators use a religious frame of reference in retrospect to explain and rationalize the atrocities of the genocide; and second, to illustrate how religious concepts of confession and forgiveness are used to deal with these post-genocide layers of conflict. Here, some of the excerpts of testimonies of one hundred thirty-eight perpetrators who were interviewed by this author in the twelve major prisons in Rwanda in 2004 will be used to illustrate how perpetrators frame and address the conflict through religious lenses. In other words:

- how perpetrators rationalize their individual and collective responsibility, and

- how the concepts of confession and forgiveness are being used to deal with the various levels of conflict as described above.

THE GENOCIDE

After Rwanda's independence, Gregoire Kayibanda's government of the first republic continued with the racial branding of the colonial era, but this time around, the policies were reversed for the benefit of the "majority"—the Hutu. In response to an attack by Rwandan exiles from Burundi in 1964, Kayibanda warned rather prophetically that if the

---

16. Linden, *Church and Revolution in Rwanda*; Mamdani, *When Victims Become Killers*.

17. Rittner, Roth, and Whitworth, *Genocide in Rwanda*; Kubai, "Being Church in Post-Genocide Rwanda"; Kubai, "Post-Genocide Rwanda"; Kubai, "Walking a Tightrope"; Longman, *Christianity and Genocide in Rwanda*.

18. Lyons and Straus, *Intimate Enemy*; Hatzfeld, *Machete Season*.

refugees attacked again, there would be a "total and summary end of the Tutsi race."[19] In these words, one can say, the president acknowledged that an ineluctable juggernaut was in motion. It was only a matter of time.

Juvenal Habyarimana's government,[20] i.e., the second republic, continued to harp on the racial differences between the Hutu and the Tutsi and continued to remind the majority that they had suffered under *alien* (Tutsi) rulers for many years. Social distinctions had become inverted and now the identity of the majority was being defined by denial of the existence of the Tutsi. The quota system, introduced by the previous regime to tackle the "problem of monopoly by Tutsi" and also eradicate official exclusion of Hutus from private and public sector, was bolstered to serve exactly the same purpose—the exclusion of the Tutsi.

It is instructive to note that this very phrase—"victims of institutional discrimination"—had been used to describe the position of the Hutu vis-à-vis the Tutsi during the period before 1959. But now, with the inversion of the same old psychocultural images, emanating from the fossilized Hamitic and other myths,[21] the majority Hutu believed that they had finally reclaimed their rightful place in Rwanda. It was felt that there was an imminent threat of the Tutsi coming back to power, so the Habyarimana government developed and fortified "Hutu Power" which was to become the rallying call or slogan during the genocide.

19. Chrétien, *The Great Lakes of Africa*, 306.

20. Juvenal Habyarimana came to power in 1973 through a coup d'état.

21. The Hamitic hypothesis is traced to the Judaic and Christian myths of biblical times (Gen 10:6ff.). The biblical narrative links Egypt with the children of Ham. However, it was after Napoleon's 1798 expedition to Egypt that the Hamitic myth was turned upside down (Mamdani, *When Victims Become Killers*, 81–86) and all signs of civilization in Africa came to be attributed to mobile Hamitic conquerors and rulers, who were believed to have descended from a superior, perhaps a lost Caucasian race. Consequently, physical features became the single most important mark of differentiation between the "Negroes" and the "Hamites" in Africa. To the latter, was attributed "finer features" (angular faces, aquiline noses, and tallness) though with a brown skin, and of course, a much higher intelligence than the "Negroes." The Hamitic myth was incarnated in the second half of the nineteenth century after the famous explorer John Hannington Speke produced an awesome account of the landscape of Rwanda. To explain the presence of elaborate monarchical systems in this region, he set forth a theory of an ancient invasion by the Galla from Ethiopia. It is important to mention this here because this theory played an important role in the formulation of the Tutsi *alien* identity which was to shape the history of this little country and its people.

Therefore the genocide was "not an eruption of ancient tribal hatreds . . . rather, this was a planned coordinated, directed, controlled attack."[22] The "genocide was orchestrated by an authoritarian and highly centralized state and abetted by a culture of passive obedience."[23] It was the culmination of a long process that entailed the institutionalization of overt discrimination and exclusion of one group by the *other*. At the core of this process was the question of relations between these identity groups. Through "racist propaganda and militarization of society, Rwandan society moved towards genocide."[24] The shooting down in Kigali of the plane with both the Rwandan (Habyarimana) and Burundian (Ntaryamira) presidents was the cue to start a well-planned extermination of one section of the Rwanda population. In a period of three months, beginning April 1994, Rwanda lost more than a million people in mass killings, a genocide of unparalleled proportions.[25]

It is not the intention here to present a history of the genocide, suffice it to say that, the Rwandan "conflict is historically entrenched, running through the pre-colonial, colonial and post colonial periods. It is embedded in myth, legend, contested histories, and animosities between Rwandans . . ."[26] Rwanda was said to be the most Catholic country in Africa with 90 percent of the population professing Christianity and "Catholicism . . . completely enmeshed in Rwandese society from top to bottom."[27] The Church had gradually become the most important social institution. One scholar comes to the conclusion that: "After all, but for the army and the Church, the two prime movers, the two organizing and leading forces, one located in the state and the other in the society, there would have been no genocide."[28] This succinctly sums up the role of the church in the genocide, and therefore, the society's recourse to re-

22. Jones, *Peacemaking in Rwanda*, 39.

23. UN Rwanda, "United Nations Development Assistance Framework," 4.

24. Uvin, *Aiding Violence*, 53.

25. Gérard Prunier notes that it is absolutely impossible to produce an accurate figure for those killed in the Rwandese genocide. Many weak, old people, and children died of sheer exhaustion, starvation, and disease during the long and dangerous trek as they fled to the neighboring countries. Only an estimate is possible. Prunier, *The Rwandan Crisis*.

26. Villa-Vicencio, *Building Nations*, 73.

27. Prunier, *The Rwandan Crisis*, 34.

28. Mamdani, *When Victims Become Killers*, 233.

ligion in dealing with the aftermath is well within the Rwandan religious psyche, so to say.

We also note that, though the Rwandan genocide fits well with other cases of genocide during the twentieth century, where ideology and state roles are key to the occurrence of genocide, it "was horrific even by the standards of a century repeatedly marred by mass political and ethnic slaughters . . . mass genocide found its most brutally efficient expression to date in Rwanda."[29] Rwandan genocide is different in several important respects:

- No sophisticated weaponry or gas chambers were used to kill. In some cases soldiers and others who had access to guns and hand grenades were called upon as reinforcements when large numbers of Tutsi were assembled together in churches or other places.

- It was largely close one-to-one combat.

- No one killed an unknown stranger—in the case of unknown persons, effort was made to ascertain whether they were Tutsi or Hutu.

- People killed friends and family—the definition of "enemy" as being "cockroaches" and "snakes" was extended to include family members who were considered to have "Tutsi blood."

Over a long period, the Hamitic ideology had been broken down to what I would call "digestible" particles for the masses of the Rwandan population. From a psychological point of view, Böhm makes an important observation that "the perpetrator develops via preparation, group identity, dilution of responsibility in the act he commits, and there by perverting his views on human relations."[30] However, though this is true for Rwanda, we need to look beyond the questions of human relations and responsibility to see how the concept of *enemy* and imagery of Tutsi as cockroach was understood in the cultural context, for instance, by mothers who killed their own children, brothers-in-law who killed their nephews and nieces; people who killed their spouses and friends in "a genocide of unparalleled proportions."[31]

---

29. Jones, *Peacemaking in Rwanda*, 1.

30. Böhm, "Psychoanalytic Aspects," 8.

31. Gourevitch, *We Want to Inform You*, 133.

"EVEN GOD KNEW . . . IT WAS GOD'S CASE"

In the following, a few excerpts from interviews with prisoners in Rwanda are presented in order to illustrate their rationalization of their acts. First, is an interview with a male prisoner serving a twenty-five year jail term in Kibungo Central prison. He gives a detailed account of his participation in the genocide.

> I have spent 7 years in prison and I am 39 years old. I am a married man with 5 children. I am charged with crimes against humanity. My own role in the 1994 genocide is evident. In other words, I don't shy away from the fact that I participated in the genocide . . .
>
> It should be remembered that in the villages, there were some Tutsi who were married to Hutus and they were still alive. So an order came out that no Tutsi should survive whether married to Hutu or not. On that day we went on a hunt and I think we killed about eight Tutsi. And killing of Tutsi in our village, (*secteur*), was done in one day—16th April 1994. Some had escaped earlier on, but I am sure they died somewhere else. For us, we took only two days to finish the Tutsi. And the Tutsi really died so badly. They were first tortured before they died. They would first make their victims run all around as they beat them up and so on. I tell the truth because if I don't, God will blame me. We were taught that the Tutsi were bad and indeed we hated them . . .
>
> This thing made me angry, to assure you, I started to hate the Tutsi with all my heart. I even told the survivors that I killed them when I hated them. I had gone to Gacaca courts in my village and told them the truth of the matter. They [the survivors] also acknowledged that I was the only prisoner telling the truth. They even gave me sugar saying that even though I killed their people, I deserve something for the truth I was telling. I was telling them the truth that I had hated them. I further went to tell them that they should continue thanking God because they are still alive.
>
> Otherwise, during genocide I had become so bad and I felt like killing all the Tutsi, to be sincere. And I have a reason not to hide this. I remember when I was in exile in Tanzania, I would always have the bad memories in me. Even now when I remember what happened, I feel like crying. I remember the family of Munyaneza and all those others we killed and feel touched . . . When I was in Tanzania I started regretting why I killed the family of Munyaneza. But I would console myself that it was God's case . . .

So one day, a religious person came into our prison and asked me to think about confessing before God. I took a first chance, stood before people in my home area and testified about all that I had done. But this testimony was in a sense of respecting God. But up to now, I tell my God that "I did everything when you knew and I therefore ask you to take charge of everything ... I called for the Prosecutor—state attorney—and at first they refused me to see him. But when I met him, I told him that I wanted to meet those that I wronged so that I can ask them to forgive me ...

When I was going to greet Fredrick, I remembered that I last met him in 1994 when he told me that "I now know the hunted. It is the Tutsi." Those were the last words I had heard from him. I even feared shaking hands with him. But it was him who started the greeting: "how are you?" He gave me his hand to shake and I actually thought that he was deceiving me ... He finally asked me if I was ready to tell him or answer his questions. I told him that I would tell him all that I knew. And the first question was "why did you kill my mother?" I explained to him as it happened. What didn't you really get from our home?" He asked the second question. I answered that it was the work of Satan since I got everything I wanted ... I asked him to forgive me. I went further to ask to know if he really forgave me. But he told me to wait until further notice.

I later got a chance to go to my *secteur* where I committed the offences. Many people gathered—survivors, returnees, etc. I knelt before them and confessed all I did in the 1994 genocide. And everyone commented that if all prisoners were like me Rwanda would be peaceful. The prosecutor asked Fredrick: "this man is asking you to forgive him. Have you done so?" Fredrick stood up and said "Gite wronged me, killed my people and the people of Rwanda. He thought of asking for forgiveness and I will also think of forgiving him." So I went back to prison and later on I appeared in court where they told me that according to my offenses I was supposed to be with people in category 1. But because I confessed I would appear in category 2, I was thus sentenced to 25 years in prison which I am now serving. This is how I joined genocide and this is how I committed the crimes.

But before God now, I am innocent. God forgave me. There is a Kinyaruanda proverb which says that Rwandans never tell the truth. But really in my morning prayers and evening prayers, I don't forget all those I wronged. I don't mind about those who made me go to prison because if I had not wronged them, I wouldn't have been accused. In short, this is the way I behaved in period of genocide.[32]

Following below is an excerpt of an interview with a perpetrator in Remera Central Prison, Kigali.

"IF YOU TRY TO FIND OUT THE REASON AS TO WHY WE KILLED, IT IS LIKE SATAN WAS WITH US"

And in no time, the "responsible" came back with soldiers and ordered us to hunt the Tutsi. The soldiers left without a word. "If we find a person who has not killed, he is going to suffer," ordered our responsible. We immediately got the Tutsi and started killing them with hoes and other sharp instruments and weapons. But those who were with us had escaped after hearing the orders we were being given. They joined others in a playground.

In fact, my role is that I personally killed two Tutsi. If you try to find out the reason as to why we killed, it is like Satan was with us, but had passed through our leaders. I killed my victims with the lower part of a spear. You know you just put a spear upside down and use it. I killed one before the eyes of his family and I buried him there. I killed the other on the side of the road and buried him there, too. But I had picked that one from a nearby bar, where he had just told the owner of the bar to give him some beer to drink, since he was going to be killed anyway. He was given two bottles of the local beer, which he drunk and we took him where he met his death. The massacres were ordered by the leaders because the president died on 6th and we started killing on 8th after getting orders from authorities. Otherwise, I even went to my home area and asked the women whose husbands I killed to forgive me and some were positive. Now I feel relieved

. . .

Another horrifying situation about which I may tell you is that of a woman whom they beat and almost crushed her head and left her for dead. But she wasn't dead yet. Another day there came a man demanding money from her, when she could produce any, he beat her to death. I told the court exactly this and implicated this man because he demanded the money and killed the woman in my presence. He in fact subjected the woman to one of the worst tortures that made her die in deep pain. And that is why I confessed and am able to testify even today. Before they would give me the sacrament, I had to clean my soul.

32. Interview, Kibungo Central Prison, June 27, 2004.

And now I feel that the country will be united, only that we have some rumors that there is some insurgence looming. But we don't believe it to be true. I don't think what happened will happen again because even if you gave me a machete to kill, I won't. What I did taught me a lesson. I only served in one republic, but see what I did. We however need very much to change the hate ideology as the president normally says.[33]

A third testimony, this time of a female prisoner, in Nsinda Central Prison, is here presented.

I went into exile in 1994 in Tanzania, where we stayed until we came back. When I reached home, I was arrested and jailed. A woman was accusing me of having killed her daughter. When the prosecutor asked whether I accept the charge, I refused. I was too afraid to tell the truth. Instead, I said that the woman was accusing me because of land wrangles since she was my neighbor. We were later transferred to Byumba, where they continued to teach us how to confess and tell the truth. I was jailed in 1996, but I revealed the truth in 1998. But some people with whom I was jailed still refuse to tell the truth, up to now. At first, I would tell half the truth and dodge other facts, until I became confident. They would tell us that this is the government of national unity, telling us what is good; and that, if that bad government advised people to kill, why don't we take good advice. Confessing and asking for forgiveness demands a lot of courage and prayers.

I was accused of killing my neighbor . . . There was one Gasangwa who was my neighbor. We had no problem in fact we would share banana juice, his wife was my friend. We were close neighbors. It was one Thursday when I woke up at about six in the morning and found that he had come to take refuge in my home. But before that, a day after Habyarmana died, we saw smoke everywhere, noise. We heard that they were slaughtering Tutsi and others are taking refuge in Bishops' homes and the church. So the man asked me to hide him. I hid him. But the next day, I ordered him to go and hide somewhere else. He begged to be allowed to stay since there was no man to kill him. But I insisted that he go. I had a neighbor who was an Interahamwe.[34] I went to tell him that Gasangwa was in my home. He advised me to go and keep him busy as he organized the killers. But when I came back, Gasangwa had disappeared through the back door.

33. Interview, Remera Central Prison, Kigali, May 26, 2004.

34. Interahamwe were Hutu militia groups.

When the Interahamwe came, they found that he had already disappeared. He was however captured on the second day and killed. Those who killed him were lucky, they were released.

I continued to have a desire in me to confess and ask that old woman to forgive me. That man was really my friend and he would have sought refuge anywhere. The fact that I called his killers is a great shame to me. So the woman accuses me of having surrendered her son, which I accept.

When I arrived here, God's word touched me and I managed to confess, accept all that I did and ask for forgiveness. I didn't kill my neighbor. Very many women here in prison didn't join the attacking groups, but directed them, searched for victims and looted. But even that is a crime enough. What if I had not shouted, Gasangwa may be alive. As we trekked into refuge, all along the way we passed very many dead bodies. I have now spent 9 years in prison.

During the genocide, things were so frightening, you could see your friend, neighbor, is being led to die. In short, it is Satan that came to us and sowed hatred in people. We only ask God not to witness the same again. We recently watched on the television how people were saving other people's lives. It makes me regret why couldn't hide that man in the same way. It is shameful to see that a woman cannot save a person from death, while women in our culture are regarded as good.

The only thing I ask is the government to make it possible for me to go and see that old woman I betrayed. Our children used to share food, play together, etc. To see that I did this, I want to ask them to forgive me, it was Satan. She may or may not forgive me because I really wronged her and it is her right. Saying it has in itself helped me before they raise the issue and make me hopeless, with my head bent down. But now at 46 years, I feel a little confident.[35]

Below follows a short excerpt of a testimony given by a male prisoner in Nsinda Central Prison.

I was jailed in 1994 and I am now 46 years old. There was a man that I killed in the company of other men. It was very early in the morning when they picked me up from home, accusing me of not taking part in the then night patrols. They sent me and others to go and fetch that man. We brought him and they went to kill

---

35. Interview, Ndinda Central Prison, June 12, 2004.

him. What I heard though I was not there was that they dumped him in a pit that was dug when they were looking for minerals.

The government is to blame for what happened, because they could have stopped it if they wanted. The government assured the people that the Tutsi invader was their enemy and deserved death for the (people's) own good. At the time of the genocide, I was 39 years old and that Tutsi we killed for example was our good neighbor. I didn't participate in any other attack. I only stayed at Musha where I was working for a Bishop. As it is well known, of course, very many people died in churches. You know before Satan entered into the people's minds, churches were good places for hiding. As a person who is born again, I confessed so that even if I die, my life, my spirit, is received in heaven. And of course another fact is that when you testify, your sentence is reduced. I am now feeling fine.

Finally an excerpt is here presented from an interview with a perpetrator in Rilima Central Prison.

I was put in jail in 1996, charged with participation in the 1994 Rwandan genocide. But actually, we the poor peasants just found ourselves in the acts of genocide unknowingly. It was the work of the leaders but unfortunately, even us, the poor, are implicated.

The war, killings, etc., were started by leaders and if they had not wanted it, they would have stopped it. It is difficult to tell what brought about the hatred. But because, or as Adam and Eve went to the forbidden Garden of Eden, being used by Satan, we too got involved in the killings as Adam and Eve got into the garden. It was the work of Satan. So we killed those people and we were put in prison and now time has come to reveal the truth and what we did. Such is the trend.

I joined in two main attacks. In the first one, we went and killed a man and in the second, we killed three. The first man was killed in a house, but we killed the other three in a valley. We used traditional weapons to kill them. We put all those we killed in a pit latrine. When we were killing those people, it seemed that we had lost the sense of humanity. Otherwise, how do you just kill someone without any reason, someone who does not even owe you anything? This shows the stupidity with which we killed the Tutsi. This is why I have decided to testify and reveal what happed and who actually did it.

The people we killed were not strangers, they were our friends, neighbors, etc. I come from the commune Gashora, but to assure you, during that time, nobody had a say (I mean the masses). It was only the leaders who dictated. And had the leaders wanted to stop the genocide, they would have done it. When I decided to testify, I first asked God to forgive me and then the people I wronged. The survivors promised to forgive me, and the situation in which I am now, is a bit promising—that is after testifying. You know I am a Muslim and it is believed that Muslims didn't participate much in the genocide. But I think this is wrong because I am a typical example. Nevertheless, I had just joined Islam. Yes people didn't die only in churches, there are some Tutsi who had taken refuge in our Mosque, but they were burnt inside. Otherwise, Rwandans can live peacefully again because it is all the work of the government, "tell people to do good, they will, and tell them to kill, they will."[36]

DISCUSSION

The above excerpts of testimonies present the perpetrators' own constructions of the genocide, the apparent gaps or inconsistency in the narratives can be attributed to the fact that they are given after a number of years of incarceration; and also that they depended on the extent to which an individual perpetrator can reconstruct the events that took place in the specific places where they were. As said above, the larger study of which this chapter is a part, is based on one hundred thirty eight testimonies recorded in all major prisons in Rwanda, representing a cross section of perpetrators who had confessed, both male and female and of all religious persuasions. Like Lyons and Straus suggest, testimonies offer an unmitigated view of the perpetrators of genocide, their fears and their choices.[37] For our purpose, a key observation is that the perpetrators made a choice that they later attributed to the influence of Satan. In one of the last testimonies, the perpetrator introduces an interesting point that the churches were good before Satan entered people's minds. Considering that thirty of the largest massacres took place in churches, it is instructive to note that killing in the churches is attributed to the influence of Satan.

Furthermore, in the testimonies, the perpetrators did not make explicit reference to the Hamitic theory or Tutsi "alienness." Most of them said that they killed their "enemy, the Tutsi," on government orders; they said that their relations had changed and they hated the Tutsi, *Inyenzi*

36. Interview, Rilima Prison, June 26, 2004.
37. Lyons and Straus, *Intimate Enemy*.

(cockroaches). Following the death of President Habyariamana, it was necessary to kill the *Inyenzi*, it was the work of Satan. After all, God knew about these things, it was said.

When the perpetrators are troubled by the horror of their actions, they turn to religion. They confess to crimes of genocide and "reveal the truth" of what they did and many of them say that they feel better, "relieved" after that. Thus confession helped in these cases the individual to be restored emotionally and psychologically, though they admit that "confessing and asking for forgiveness demands a lot of courage." Through confession and forgiveness, religion provided a way of dealing with feelings of guilt, shame and fear for both the victim and victimizer. Confession gave the female perpetrator in Nsida prison hope and confidence to face the society. This is also evident when, for instance, the interviewee Gite meets Fredrick whose mother he killed: the tension is palpable, but they manage to shake hands and Gite asks for forgiveness. Acknowledgement of responsibility and guilt is generally speaking important for the victims even if it does not take away the pain and loss. More importantly, acknowledgement provides the space on which both perpetrator and survivor/victim can stand, reflect on the genocide and interrogate the relationship with each other.

They also believe that God has forgiven them, as the Kibungo prison perpetrator says above, "before God now I am innocent. God forgave me"; while the one in Remera prison says it was necessary to clean his soul before taking the sacrament. They get consolation from the belief that even if God knew that genocide would take place. But it was the work of Satan. When they ruminate on the causes of the conflict, they acknowledge the hatred they had for the Tutsi: one perpetrator says he hated the Tutsi with all his heart and therefore he killed them; and another one says "we were taught that the Tutsi were bad and indeed we hated them"; while yet another posits that "It is difficult to tell what brought about the hatred."

There is no doubt, the challenges of post-genocide Rwanda are enormous and call for extraordinary responses. The extension of the definition of the cockroaches and the enemy to members of one's own family, as a prisoner once said in an interview that "One could kill sons or daughters; his family was not safe, so long as there was Tutsi blood somewhere, somehow,"[38] sets the Rwandan genocide apart. And now

38. Interview, Rilima Central Prison, June 26, 2004.

many Rwandans say "it is difficult to live with what we know." But as said above, they must find a way of not only living together, but also of living with what they know about their history.

For Rwandans in general, one of the ways in which to deal with this complex situation was to turn to God, thus religious concepts have come to play a central role as they have become mainstreamed in the reconstruction policy. Confession and forgiveness become crucial for the national policy on unity and reconciliation.[39] Thus religious ideas have been used to provide the framework,[40] both in theory and practice, for the peace processes on which the both the government and individuals bank the hope of creating a harmonious society where victim/survivor and perpetrator live side by side, without the desire for revenge and a sense of guilt and shame respectively. The *gacaca* is a concrete example of how confession and forgiveness have been used to reduce the congestion in the prisons, and more importantly to create the space for perpetrators and victims to speak the unspeakable truth of the horror of genocide.

According to the New Testament, Satan is not simply a mythological name for the impersonal fact of evil. Satan is here encountered in a human form, a conscious power with a will, purpose, and the ability to exercise influence. A question this raises is why a satanic discourse has assumed such prominence, in the explanation of genocide among the perpetrators? Why is it that perpetrators seek to attribute their own actions to the work of Satan? Perhaps this Satan discourse provides the lens through which the horrors of genocide can be meaningfully interpreted and/or rationalized. This discourse provides a theory of supernatural agency which can plausibly be blamed for the genocide and the ghastly manner in which individual perpetrators carried out killing of the victims. Thus the "work of Satan" can explain not just the acts of individual perpetrators, but also those of the government which planned and executed the genocide. It is a way of suppressing a sense of individual responsibility; in other words, a form of externalization of responsibility for the wanton massacre of neighbors, friends, and even

39. Kubai, "Between Justice and Reconciliation."

40. The *gacaca* justice system on which hinges the process of justice and reconciliation and ultimately national social and economic development is a reinvention of traditional practice of community justice, based on traditional values and norms. Central to the *gacaca* are concepts of confession and forgiveness.

family. As the prisoner in Remera prison, Kigali, says above: "if you try to find out the reason as to why we killed, it is like Satan was with us, but had passed through our leaders." Religion played an important role in shaping the history of Rwanda, therefore the use of a religious frame of reference by the perpetrators and the appropriation of religious concepts for the purpose of post-genocide social reconstruction, strike a familiar cord in a society that is still largely religious.

The confession of crimes, which individual perpetrators committed or witnessed during the genocide, became crucial to the issue of justice for perpetrators. The government created incentives to encourage perpetrators to come out and tell the truth. It was stipulated that those who confessed and assisted with investigations would benefit from a reduction in jail sentence when time came for them to be tried. For instance, if the maximum sentence, for a crime an individual was accused of, was ten years, and if such an individual confessed and was deemed to be genuine, the sentence would be commuted to half—the person would instead serve five years. As a result of this initiative and the work of religious organizations and actors such as Prison Fellowship Rwanda chaplains and their message that the prisoners could be forgiven of their crimes if they confessed and asked for forgiveness, many prisoners confessed and asked to be forgiven.[41]

Having suffered untold pain and loss, survivors viewed this as an injustice to them, but we shall not pursue this line of argument here, the point is to illustrate how the government resorted to confession as a means of reintegrating the perpetrators into the society. In the excerpts of the testimonies presented above, the perpetrators say that they wanted to meet their victims face to face and ask for forgiveness. After they are forgiven, they feel better, they "can sleep well" or experience some sort of "inner peace" or "confidence." The victims/survivors are obliged to forgive those who beg for forgiveness, again this requirement has its challenges, but in the face of the greater threat of revenge, fear, and guilt confession becomes an important resource for the greater good of making it possible for victim and victimizer to live together. It helps create a sense of optimism expressed in the words of the perpetrator in Remera prison: "And now I feel that the country will be united . . . We however, need very much to change the hate ideology as the president normally says."

41. Samset and Kubai, *Evaluation of Released Prisoners' Project.*

BIBLIOGRAPHY

Böhm, Tomas. "Psychoanalytic Aspects on Perpetrators in Genocide: Experiences from Rwanda." *Scandinavian Psychoanalytic Review* 29 (2006) 22–33.

Chrétien, Jean-Pierre. *The Great Lakes of Africa: Two Thousand Years of History.* New York: Zone, 2003.

"Genocide Ideology and the Strategies for Its Eradication." Senate Commission Report. Kigali: Government of Rwanda, 2006.

Gourevitch, Philip. *We Wish to Inform You That Tomorrow We Will be Killed With Our Families.* London: Picador, 2000.

Hatzfeld, Jean. *Machete Season: The Killers in Rwanda Speak.* New York: Farrar, Straus, and Giroux, 2003.

Jha, Uma Shanker, and Surya Narayan Yadav. *Rwanda: Towards Reconciliation, Good Governance and Development.* Delhi: Association of Indian Africanist, n.d.

Jones, Bruce D. *Peacemaking in Rwanda.* London: Lynne Rienner, 2001.

Kaplan, Suzanne. *Children in Genocide.* London: Internationals Psychoanalytical Association, 2009.

Kubai, Anne N. "Being Church in Post-Genocide Rwanda: The Challenges of Forgiveness and Reconciliation." In *On Being Church: African Women's Voices and Visions,* edited by Isabel Apawo Phiri and Sarojini Nadar, 96–127. Geneva: World Council of Churches, 2005.

———. "Between Justice and Reconciliation: The Survivors of Rwanda." *African Security Review* 16/1 (2007) 53–66.

———. "Gacaca and Post-Genocide Reconstruction in Rwanda." In *Indigenous Voices in the Sustainability Discourse,* edited by Frans Wijsen and Sylvia Marcos, 260–80. Berlin: LIT, 2010.

———. "Living in the Shadow of Genocide: Women and HIV/AIDS in Rwanda." In *Women, Religion and HIV/AIDS in Africa,* edited by Teresia Hinga et al, 49–74. Durban, South Africa: Cluster, 2008.

———. "Post-Genocide Rwanda: The Changing Religious Landscape." *Exchange: Journal of Missiological and Ecumenical Research* 36/2 (2007) 198–214.

———. "Walking a Tightrope: Muslims and Christian in Rwanda." *Islam and Christian-Muslim Relations* 18/2 (2007) 219–35.

Linden, Ian. *Church and Revolution in Rwanda.* Manchester: Manchester University Press, 1997.

Longman, Timothy. *Christianity and Genocide in Rwanda.* New York: Cambridge University Press, 2010.

Lyons, Robert, and Scott Straus. *Intimate Enemy: Images and Voices of the Rwandan Geno-cide.* New York: Zed, 2006.

Mamdani, Mahmood. *When Victims Become Killers: Colonialism, Nativism, and the Genocide in Rwanda.* Kampala: Fountain, 2001.

Power, Samantha. *A Problem From Hell: America and the Age of Genocide.* New York: New Republic, 2002.

Prunier, Gérard. *The Rwandan Crisis: History of Genocide.* Kampala: Fountain, 1999.

Rittner, Carol, John K. Roth, and Wendy Whitworth, eds. *Genocide in Rwanda: Complicity of the Churches?* St. Paul, MN: Paragon House, 2004.

Samset, Ingrid, and Anne N. Kubai. *Evaluation of Released Prisoners' Project in Rwanda: Field Research Report.* Oslo: Norwegian Church Aid, 2005.

UN Rwanda. "United Nations Development Assistance Framework" (UNDAF). Kigali: Rwanda, August 2000.

Uvin, Peter. *Aiding Violence: The Development Enterprise in Rwanda.* West Hartford, CT: Kumarian, 1998.

Villa-Vicencio, Charles. *Building Nations: Transitional Justice in the African Great Lakes Region.* Cape Town: Institute for Justice and Reconciliation, 2005.

5

In Search of Grace

Religion and the ELN

Jennifer Schirmer

The final destiny of humanity was the revolution. It held the same version of sacredness as the religions, but with paradise here on earth. At its base, the revolution followed the religious concept disguised as earthliness . . . we [the ELN] did not kill the Christian idealism, we edited it into a form of revolutionary idealism . . .[1]

If we are to learn whether and how a set of religious beliefs can take hold and influence a particular guerrilla movement, we need to ask ourselves several questions: In what way might religion serve in a guerrilla movement? Might revolution serve as a religion for such a group? Is a revolutionary priest an oxymoron? By focusing on the Colombian guerrilla group, *Ejército de Liberación Nacional*, Army of National Liberation (ELN), we can at least begin to develop some insights about these questions.

In much of the literature on religion and conflict, as well as on insurgent movements, we find rather stylized, even binary, categories of thought: it is either religion or revolution. This approach is problematic

1. Correa, "Comentario," 90. "I cannot think of anything more religious as image and as symbol, than the image of January 1959 in Havana with Fidel, with his beard and the white dove on his houlder. That is pure Christianity of redemption . . . The image of the heroic guerrillero, with a face like Christ . . . a star with a beret. If this is not Christianity, then I don't know what religion is" (Broderick, "Ponencia," 34–35). All translations from Spanish to English are made by the author.

because even if it's not a religious conflict per se, the interface between religion and revolutionary fervor and beliefs may be influential in terms of recruitment, commitment, and perhaps most especially, identity.

The ELN guerrilla movement in Colombia is a case in point. As a quasi-religious insurgent group, the combination of Catholicism and socialism produced a blend of faith, sacrifice and *entrega* (a mission, a dedication) that is impressive in its critical amalgam of both revolutionary ideology and religious fervor—*without being part of any political party or church*. This sense of mission allows us to better understand how much the vocabulary and commitment of some revolutionary movements may be rooted in religion even if they are not "religious" in a conventional sense.

Despite Colombia being a very Catholic country and despite the Cuban model adopted by the ELN being "Jesuitical" in its character,[2] religion per se did not visibly play a role in the early years of the ELN. It was not until *after* the death of Father Camilo Torres Restrepo, a high-profile ordained Catholic priest who left the Church to ferment a radical socialist movement, *Frente Unido* (United Front), that religion became a more visible element of ELN ideology. With his joining the ELN and his early death in combat in 1966, the radical pastoral aspects of liberation theology, a theology that was taking hold among seminarians throughout Europe and Latin America at the time, took root within the ELN rather unexpectedly. This, in turn, opened the guerrilla organization not only to students, peasants, and workers but recruits from seminaries as well as ordained priests and nuns. Indeed, a number of priests and seminarians would serve in future as leaders and commanders in the ELN in the 1980s and 1990s.

As we shall see, since the 1960s, the ELN, although not a religious movement per se, represents an interesting amalgam of beliefs that helped serve in recruitment, commitment, and identification of a revolutionary belief and ritual. This, in turn, has served as an important counterpoint for the last forty plus years, to the predominant model of Left revolution in Colombia: the Communist Party and its military complement, the FARC guerrillas.

---

2. As one former *fidelista* remarked, "Fidel's early speeches were curious to me as a Catholic schoolgirl in Havana, and then I realized what it was: of course! He was trained by the Jesuits and he spoke in threes!" (personal remarks, Paris, January 2012).

Thus, today, the centrality of religious belief in the ELN may make a difference in how the ELN would like to be remembered, were it to negotiate a peace settlement under the current President Juan Manuel Santos. Indeed, the broader question is, does an amalgam of radical Catholic and Marxist belief make a negotiated peace more possible?

Before we undertake the discussion of religion and the ELN, it is important to set out the ELN's history.

THE BIRTH AND EVOLUTION OF THE ELN IDEOLOGY

Cuban Foco—Fidelista-Guevarista

Some analysts argue that the beginnings of the ELN can be found in Cuba in 1963 based as it is on the principle of the Cuban revolution: *castrismo* with its *foquismo* and *voluntarismo* in which actions of professional revolutionaries serve as the impulse for revolutionary processes.

> Indeed, religion had little role in the initial thinking associated with the ELN. Marx and Lenin replaced the Christian God . . . Latin Americans substituted Castro and Che as Christ Redeemed . . . they were deified with their own martyrs and Ten Commandments.[3]

The Cuban model also represented an important rupture of the military-political split of traditional communist parties. Rather than a separation between the military and the political, these two elements of revolutionary practice were unified. Inspired by Fidel's and Che's success[4] and doctrine, seven men formed *Brigada Pro-liberación de Colombia Jose Antonio Galán* in Cuba in 1963, named in honor of the assassinated radical liberal-populist leader. It proposed to return to Colombia to organize the revolutionary fight militarily and politically simultaneously.

Once in Colombia, this Brigade was transformed into the National Liberation Army (ELN), with the Manifesto of Simacota in 1965, inaugurating a vision of revolution in contrast to that of the Communist Party, which had, up until this time, represented "the Left" in Colombia.

The Manifesto of Simacota reflected not only the Cuban revolutionary experience, but also the Colombian legacies of *La Violencia* in

---

3. Correa, "Comentario," 89.

4. See Burgos on how this "success" based on little armed action was transplanted to the rest of Latin America as a revolutionary model, in some interpreters' eyes "recklessly" (Burgos, "L'Operation Pedro Pan").

the 1950s. The ELN was established in Santander in the very same zones of the earlier radical liberal guerrillas, led by Rafael Rangel.[5] They were guerrillas who had been organized around the concept of self-defense against the Conservative Party-controlled and brutally repressive police forces. Some analysts argue that these early forms of "radical liberalism" had as much, if not more, to do with the ideological formation of these latter-day guerrillas, as did the Cuban and Chinese revolutions.[6] Moreover, Santander, known for its difficult terrain, was topographically ideal for *una guerra de guerrillas*, a war of guerrillas. It also allowed for control of the richest oil fields in the country, the railroad of Magdalena and the largest workers' movement in the nation. In addition, some of the Brigade already had contacts with the radical industrial university union.[7]

Other Ideological Influences: The Sino Epoch

Apart from the Cuban model, the other international influences emerged from the Sino-Soviet splits within the Colombian Communist Party itself. Radically confronting the orthodoxy of the traditional communist parties, the Chinese faction fought against "the imperialists," led by the U.S., and focused on Africa, Asia, and Latin America through student movements, intellectuals, and trade unions. Peasant groups, however, were mostly marginalized from this debate.

In Colombia, this new approach encouraged a growing number of revolutionaries to question the platform and methods of the Communist Party, leading to a split and creation of the Communist Party Marxist-Leninist (PCm-l) as well as the emergence of organizations, such as the *Movimiento Obrero Estudiantil Campesino* (MOEC), *Las Juventudes del MRL* (JMRL), and *Movimiento Revolucionario Liberal* (MRL). This radical liberalism emerged originally from the *clase popular* of the *gaitanist* guerrillas in Barrancabermeja and San Vicente de Chucurí—gathered on the basis of revolutionary populism after the assassination of Liberal Party leader Jorge Eliécer Gaitán, in 1948.[8] This vision of *la clase popu-*

5. In this region, there did not exist *bandoleros* or bandits, who could cause confusion, as occurred in other departments. Arenas *La Guerrilla Por Dentro*, 24; cf. Molano, "Trochas y fusiles."

6. Vargas, "Anotaciones sobre el discurso ideólogico y político del ELN," 73.

7. Arenas, *La Guerrilla Por Dentro*, 24.

8. Gaitán was one of the most charismatic leaders of the Liberal Party and was as-

lar and *populismo revolucionario* was taken up again by student activist Jaime Arenas and former priest Camilo Torres and brought into the ELN in the 1960s, distinguishing it from both traditional liberalism and communism.[9]

As ELN militant Jaime Arenas explains, these "combined revolutionary lessons" from the Cuban and Chinese theoretical debates contributed to a great degree

> in gaining the consciousness and stimulating *la lucha popular*, [in] seeking new methods and forms of working, of initiating urban and country cells that would stimulate and develop the armed struggle, in one or another modality, as the principal path for taking power.[10]

These principles at once divided the Colombian Left and helped it gain a new consciousness in the 1960s.

Poor military judgments and strategies, sectarianism, dogmatism, and opportunism were to blame for the destruction of a number of revolutionary organizations during this period, including the MOEC (Movimiento Obrero Estudiantil Campesino), FUAR (Frente Unido de Acción Revolucionaria) and a number of guerrilla groups in different regions.[11] Contacts in Havana, by the leaders of the newly formed ELN (by way of a brother of one of the Brigade leaders)[12] with the *Juventudes del Movimiento Revolucionario Liberal* (The Liberal Revolutionary Movement, JMRL), led to the formation of a new grouping within Colombia, and with which the ELN decided to link itself. Arenas explains:

> [Our] intention was to provide a great impulse to this group with its network of urban combat groups with the intention of con-

---

sassinated during his second presidential campaign in 1948, setting off *El Bogotazo*: a violent period of political unrest in Colombian history known as *La Violencia* (approx. 1948 to 1958) (cf. Sharpless, *Gaitán of Colombia*). The FARC, in contrast, coming from the Communist Party, did not explicitly assume a gaitanist posture.

9. Zabala, "Comentario," 108.

10 Arenas, *La Guerrilla Por Dentro*, 19.

11. For example, guerrillas led by Antonio Larrota in the south, guerrillas led by Tulio Bayer in el Vichada, guerrillas of Federico Arango in Territorio Vasquez, guerrillas of MOEC in Uraba and Bolivar (Antioquia), guerrillas of the PC m-l in el Valle and San Pablo, together with the disappearance of FUAR, Juventudes del MRL and MOEC. Arenas, *La Guerrilla Por Dentro*.

12. Manuel Vásquez Castaño, brother of Fabio Castaño.

verting it into a political auxiliary to [our] urban and guerrilla movement . . . to work on propaganda for the guerrilla. For the ELN, it would also dedicate itself to the urban work.[13]

Despite difficulties between the two groups, Arenas admits that the ELN underestimated the political work that the JMRL did accomplish in 1964–65. He also says that the link with the university students from the Industrial University of Santander (UIS) in this period was "an important chapter in the qualitative and quantitative development of the ELN" at this stage.

The internal work of the UIS student movement was of tactical and strategic importance [in terms of] being the principal source of militants with political skills in the student movement as well as in the popular sector . . . [For] we never understood the revolutionary struggle as only guerrilla action but as the conscious and efficient utilization of all possible methods.[14]

The ELN thus helped to create *Federación Universitaria Nacional* (FUN) in October 1963, and supported their three-month strike "which favored the work of the ELN" by providing "contacts with workers and in poor neighborhoods."[15] And by the end of 1964, a small urban network functioned with the ELN in the towns of Bucaramanga, Barrancabarmeja, and San Vicente de Chucurí in Santander.

The lesson learned was for the ELN to be in direct control of this activity in the future when it set up a network of urban cells (*núcleos urbanos*), with students primarily, but also with taxi drivers, mechanics and cobblers and later with the union leader of the petroleum workers at the oil port of Barrancabarmeja.

The work with the unions in Santander was particularly difficult. Santander was political territory of the Communist Party. Open hostility was expressed with the public denunciation of four of the

13. Arenas, *La Guerrilla Por Dentro*, 25, 27. *Las Juventudes* was mostly formed by university students, together with a small part of workers and peasants. But the ELN found that this group could not count on urban combat groups, as claimed in Havana. Due to an "opportunism of its leaders, sectarianism and the use of petit-bourgeois methods such as anarchic urban terrorism—i.e., spontaneity and the use of ineffective ultra-radical revolutionary language instead of serious work of agitation"—led to a rupture between the ELN and JMRL, and some of its members joined the ELN outright. Arenas, *La Guerrilla Por Dentro*, 25, 27, 28, 39.

14. Arenas, *La Guerrilla Por Dentro*, 28, 32, 38.

15. Ibid., 48.

elenos[16] by the Colombian Communist Party as "extreme Leftists" and as "adventurers"—a denunciation that clearly did not escape military intelligence.[17] This antagonism toward the ELN expressed itself openly again in Cuba in 1964 when ELN comandante Fabio Vásquez went to Havana to seek funding and military training for its thirty combatants, and was met with hostile indifference—almost causing the termination of the guerrilla group.[18]

Arenas states:

> We had very similar points of view as to the Chinese and Cubans against imperialism and for national liberation movements, *but without converting ourselves into being dependent on anyone.* The important thing for us was to seek that which most suited the Colombian revolutionary process by applying Marxist-Leninism to the reality of the country.[19]

The ELN also developed its contacts with peasant communities in Santander

> with some experience with the armed activities, having collabo-rated previously in one or another way with the radical liberal guerrillas. For them, the struggle was not strange but it was la-tent, as the last recourse to achieve the transformation of a sys-tem which had marginalized and oppressed them for centuries.[20]

In July 1964, seventeen peasants left their homes and became part of the first *núcleo* (cell) in the mountains.

Initially then, the ELN political discourse was highly nationalist and *gaitanista*: a radical liberalism concerned with democratic partici-pation and national liberation from the corrupt oligarchs whose primary instrument of power had been repressive practices that justified armed struggle. It has also been argued that this was an attempt to adapt the Marxist discourse from Cuba into the national context, and "justify"

---

16. "Elenos"—members of the ELN.

17. Arenas, *La Guerrilla Por Dentro*, 29, 32. In 2005, the FARC of the Communist Party attacked the ELN for offering to negotiate a peace settlement with the Uribe gov-ernment ("FARC contra ELN"; "Exterminio al ELN").

18. Arenas, *La Guerrilla Por Dentro*, 56.

19. Ibid., 26; emphasis mine.

20. Ibid., 54.

the ELN's use of violence without the existence of an actual political dictator.[21]

The Manifesto of Simacota

In some respects, the hostility by the Cuban Communist Party led to the decision of the ELN leadership to stage a military action in the small town of Simacota on January 7, 1965 in order to be able to maintain its troops of thirty. They robbed 60 million pesos from the Agrarian Bank, killed six members of the armed forces and police, and captured some weapons. They also lost a combatant and had two desertions: one from the Communist Party who had infiltrated the ranks, and another who gave information to the military, causing the capture and sentencing to seventeen years of prison of two ELN guerrillas.[22]

With the Manifesto of Simacota, the ELN announced itself publicly. A history of the ELN at this stage reveals an organization that is weak and indecisive with little political or financial support from Cubans, as well as facing the hostility and infiltration of its ranks by the Colombian Communist Party (CCP).

Ideologically, the ELN attempted to break away from the orthodox and reformist CCP, and combine students', peasants', workers', and intellectuals' concerns in order to develop new formulations with a more nationalist formula, in contrast to the orthodoxy of the traditional Left. As with other guerrilla groups of this period, there was a debate between reform and revolution, and

> there was something reformist about the ELN guerrillas' proposals, although they probably wouldn't like to characterize them as such. But if one supposes that the identity of being a revolutionary was to turn to violence, to fire shots, then he who would not lay claim to revolutionary violence was [seen to be] a reformist and he who fired shots was [characterized as] a revolutionary. This is the debate that continues . . .[23]

A brief discussion of the next three decades illustrates the ELN's continued contradictory and eclectic ideological formation.

---

21. Vargas, "Anotaciones sobre el discurso ideologico y politico del ELN," 76; Concerning the Manifesto de Simacota y la Declaración Programática, see 45–46, 67–71.

22. Arenas, La Guerrilla Por Dentro, 58–59.

23. Vargas, "Anotaciones sobre el discurso ideólogico y político del ELN," 76–77.

1970s and 1980s: Peasants vs. Workers

After an initial period of expansion in the 1960s, the internal debate that centered on reform-or-revolution became increasingly circumscribed in a "Stalinist manner" with the early leadership limiting this debate through numerous internal purges and executions at their base camp in Colombia.[24] Nonetheless, an internal debate did arise between *campesinismo* and *obrerismo*. On the one side was Comandante Fabio Vásquez Castaño, trained in Cuba, focusing on peasants as the vanguard of the revolution. On the other side were the Spanish priests, Manuel Pérez and Domingo Laín, committed to the Catholic-Marxist ideology and practice of "worker priests," el *Movimiento Obrero Cristiano*, and wanted to focus on the working class as the vanguard.

The debate notwithstanding, a number of militants left the ELN during this period due to the lack of democratic discussion and fear of the purges, so much so that they are referred to as "the diaspora of the ELN."[25] Moreover, with the fall of urban networks into the hands of military intelligence, the attack and killing of the majority of the ELN leadership at Anorí and the subsequent flight of Fabio Vásquez to Cuba, the ELN reached its weakest moment and was threatened with dissolution.

It was at this moment of crisis when its more nationalist discourse was radicalized, according to some analysts, that Catholic-Marxist discourse was incorporated into the ELN, together with a more internationalized version of socialist revolution by the more Christian-trained members. The priest Manuel Pérez took over the leadership with its emphasis on "diversity in an attempt to construct consensus."

1990s Federalist vs. Caudillo

In the 1990s, the ELN restructured itself into a more liberal, federalist model in which all *frentes* and those political organizations with links to the ELN were included in the decision-making process. As a result, the process of taking decisions was slowed considerably. In short, it became a federation of "many political tendencies" united under one symbol. This federalism could be seen as historically a complete rejection of the caudillo model from the 1960s which, according to many, was the cause

24. Broderick, *El guerrillero invisible*, grippingly describes the fear of these internal purges.

25. Correa, "Comentario," 88.

of much damage to the ELN. Its federalism was distinguishing the ELN even further from the Stalinist caudillo-centered FARC.

La Union Camilista-ELN proposed a National Convention in 1996 to present its *Declaración del Tercer Congreso.* This speaks of the need "to constitute a new government of broad participation . . . We want a democratic Colombia, where everyone can speak and decide in a sovereign manner the destiny of our country." The orthodox discourse of socialism is nowhere to be found, replaced, once again, with radical liberalism. In some ways, the ideological evolution has come full circle.

Moreover, a strategy of negotiation is presented as an internal decentralized dialogue as well as a dialogue with the nation without intermediaries by which to "elaborate the bases for a political agreement of social reforms looking toward a democratization of the State and society"[26] At this time, the ELN appears to have abandoned the guerrilla-as-army, with more focus on the political spaces within the national scene, returning to its emphasis on "diversity in an attempt to construct consensus . . . of course, with the intention of leading many of these consensuses."[27]

In a sense, the ELN has tried to overcome the contradictory paths of making war while making peace, of reform and revolution at once, of its strategy of guerrilla warfare combined with the construction of consensus. As one analyst said to me ironically, "The ELN is an NGO with guns."[28]

If it is an NGO with guns, it is also quite distinct from other guerrilla groups in Colombia, and perhaps closer to guerrilla groups in Nicaragua and El Salvador in terms of the marriage of Marxism with Christianity. In effect, when Camilo Torres wrote a letter in 1965 to both the ELN and the FARC regarding his interest in joining forces with his urban political movement, *Frento Unido,* the ELN recognized that they needed Camilo's dynamism and network as well as his prestige as a priest. As we shall see, this rather eclectic ideological foundation of the ELN included a criticism of the traditional Church while embracing the humanism of a nationalist liberation theology.

26. Vargas, "Anotaciones sobre el discurso ideólogico y político del ELN," 80.

27. Ibid., 81.

28. Interview with author, Bogotá 2010.

RELIGION AND THE ELN

The Catholic Church and Camilo Torre Restrepo's Background

It was in the 1950s when the Catholic Church looked upon Latin America, with its multitudes living in misery and with its social problems, as the next arena for its social action projects in its fight against communism. Unless something was done to alleviate such misery, these masses would probably pass over "to the other side." To avoid this, a new generation of Catholic intellectuals, of which Camilo Torres Restrepo was a part, were trained at the Catholic University of Louvain in Belgium and would have access to the key positions in governments throughout Latin America. It was in Louvain, the location of the first struggles of the *Movimiento Obrero Cristiano* in the 1930s and the seat of the International Confederation of Christian Trade Unions, where the ideology of Christian Democracy was taught. A Belgian priest traveled to Rome to convince Pope Pius XI that "the biggest tragedy of the 19th century was the loss of the working class by the Church." This mistake must not happen again in Latin America, he insisted.[29] In Colombia in the 1950s, while Camilo Torres was a seminarian, this was manifested in projects for the indoctrination of the peasants. One priest in Boyacá organized a large network of broadcasting schools, with one of the most powerful signals in Latin America. These were social projects perceived of as part of the Church's struggle to gain or maintain their relations with the poor and working class, against the Communist Party and "other breaches of the established order."[30]

However, given the Colombian Catholic Church's traditional conservatism, Torres found that his compatriots in Belgium were less than enthusiastic about his proselytizing spirit and enthusiasm for Catholic doctrine, and he became, to put it somewhat mildly, disillusioned with the established church. He had come to the conclusion that the armed struggle against impoverishment was inevitable in Colombia and that it was possible to attain a great transformation of the country only from a position of power. He also had misgivings about the effectiveness of the Communist Party and about the practice of "self-defense" in Marquetalia by the Bloque Sur which would establish itself as the FARC.

29. Broderick, *Camilo*, 108.
30. Ibid., 97.

He began to focus his own efforts on a more pure politics of social mobilization and over time, he came to the conclusion that it was useless to develop a political movement without a guerrilla organization. This position was, of course, not well received by the Catholic hierarchy, and despite Torres' attempts to negotiate with the leadership, he was expelled from the church, and was made a lay person. Attracted to a "purity" of militant politics, he formed the *Frente Unido* (United Front) to recover the radical liberal tradition in Colombia which sought to deploy insurrection as a central element in a politics of popular struggle.[31]

Frente Unido

The platform of this *Frente Unido* was publicized on 22 May 1965. In it, Torres declares himself:

> a revolutionary as Colombian, as sociologist, as Christian and as priest . . . As Christian because the essence of Christianity is the love of one's fellow human being, and only by revolution can one achieve the well-being of the majority. As priest because the devotion [*entrega*] to one's fellow human being that demands the revolution is a requirement of fraternal charity that is indispensable to achieve the full fulfillment of one's mission . . . *It was a Christian imperative.*[32]

On the basis of these beliefs, Torres built a movement around himself which rapidly began to preach revolution, and attempted to develop an assembly of representatives from all political parties while being committed to the radical liberalism of the *Frente Unido*. In many ways, this paralleled the eclectic nature of an earlier ELN discourse; like the ELN, this *Frente Unido*, too, was a movement whose doctrine was in evolution, "seeking a different church."[33]

Torres, though, was not allowed to go it alone in this regard. Both the Communist Party and the Christian Democrats interfered in the *Frente Unido*, with the latter complaining that "given that Camilo Torres is no longer a priest, given his reduction of status to a layperson, then he should be treated as a simple citizen."[34] Indeed, when this mass mobili-

31. Zabala, "Comentario," 109.
32. Broderick, *Camilo*, 82–83, 85; emphasis added.
33. Ibid., 36.
34. Arenas, *La Guerrilla Por Dentro*, 94.

zation attracted the ELN leadership, its leader Fabio Vásquez sent ELN militant Jaime Arenas Reyes to accompany Camilo Torres in his political work to ensure the ELN that Torres wouldn't "fall in with bad company; e.g., socialists of the Communist Party."[35]

About this same period of time, with the bombing of Marquetelia, one of the *Répúblicas Independientes* in Tolima, in 1961, which radicalized and solidified the guerrillas of self-defense into the guerrillas of the FARC,[36] and with the refusal of the Church and military to establish a peace commission to prevent such bombing only a few days earlier, Camilo Torres became strongly attracted to the *lucha armada* (the armed struggle). He even approached the FARC, an approach that was turned away. It was then, with the publication of the ELN Manifesto of Simacota in 1965, that he discovered that a number of his companions were indeed already a part of the ELN, and the ELN, in turn, became interested in him and his militant activities in Bogotá, prompting him to join the group in the mountains.

ELN Connection

With the *Frente Unido* declaration, and his expulsion from the church, Torres began to develop a closer connection with the ELN. In his words, his work with the *Frente Unido*, which included militants from the middle class, intellectuals, students, "even some from the upper class and some military officers," represented "legal action." Legal action, though, he argued needed to be coordinated with the "clandestine action" of the ELN. Although the ELN was at this time "so small and so poorly armed, was for him [Torres] even more attractive, for its very poverty."[37] Thus Torres sought to place himself within the ELN and, in turn, the ELN opened its doors to him. Broderick argues that this entry into the insurrection led directly to "a further simplification of politics" for Torres," something more romantic, more heroic, the good-vs-the bad."[38] Torres was anxious to begin, but was warned by the ELN leadership that this was a "prolonged process" that would take time.[39] Also, the ELN told

35. Broderick, *El guerrillero invisible*, 44.

36. See Marulanda's speech, January 1999, in Broderick, *El guerrillero invisible*, 44; cf. Patiño, *Las Verdaderas Intenciones de las FARC*.

37. Broderick, *El Cura Perez*, 37.

38. Ibid., 35.

39. Arenas, *La Guerrilla Por Dentro*, 90.

Torres that if one were agitating within legal boundaries, it could not be considered a revolutionary path, and that one must seek the clandestine path. "You must make your journey [to the mountains to join the ELN], you must make yourself clandestine . . ."[40]

Thus it was, that Camilo Torres, with "his impulsive temperament" and his multitudinous political movement successfully launched only three months earlier, received orders from his commander to abandon the city immediately and incorporate himself into the guerrilla as a simple combatant. "Despite whatever doubts, the young priest responded without hesitation, and he left immediately for the mountains . . . happy, without saying goodbye to anyone."[41] His disappearance of course caused great consternation in the *Frente Unido*. But Camilo,

> unconcerned in the jungle at the side of the inflamed Fabio Vásquez and surrounded by humble peasants, was living a moment of euphoria and abnegation, of revolutionary mystique . . . experienced as faith in the future of humanity. He felt that he had discovered in the armed struggle the only path that led to redemption.[42]

His dreams were sublimated to the socialist utopia, and "within that he found a quasi-religious expression in the guerrilla."[43]

Thus, although technically no longer a priest, Camilo Torres was the very embodiment of a "revolutionary priest" to those legal political actors in the Communist Party, the Christian Democrats and the multiple sectors involved in the *Frente Unido*, as well as the clandestine guerrillas of the ELN. He came to represent at once a legal and clandestine force. But by absenting himself from the visible, legal activity by joining the ELN, the *Frente Unido*—very much identified with and dependent upon his charisma—basically fell apart, despite having an impressive and massive network in many different cities and the poor neighborhoods of Bogotá.[44] Hence, in the end, Torres was unable to achieve the unity among the diverse groupings of militants and revolutionaries that he had originally sought. One might say that once more, in the politi-

40. Ibid., 96–97.

41. Ibid.

42. Ibid., 97.

43. Broderick, *Camilo*, 171.

44. Moreover, the Communist Party sabotaged the distribution of the FU's newspaper. Arenas, *La Guerrilla Por Dentro*.

cal tradition of Colombia, "the myopia of the revolutionaries" impeded unity which could have advanced the process.[45]

A New Epoch: An Amalgam of a Different Christianity and Marxism

With the decision of priest Camilo Torres to join the ranks of the ELN in 1966, together with many other priests, seminarians, nuns, and university students, something new emerged: a period of Christianity and Marxism which had a major influence on the ideology and political practice of the ELN. Some argue that from this point forward, the ELN became the embodiment of a religious revolution.

> Camilo Torres found in the discourse of the ELN a space to participate in a process of change . . . and that the doors were opened to him to be able to manifest his revolutionary commitment.[46]

This apparently straightforward shift indicates to some that there were already strong elements of Christianity within the ELN movement. Compare this to the FARC which was also presented a letter from Torres, expressing interest, but "given the atheist nature of the FARC and the Communist Party, it was not a likely match."[47]

Distancing itself from the Colombian Communist Party's dominance, the ELN began to deploy quasi-religious symbols as an impulse to join the revolutionary fervor

> without really understanding what revolution meant. But if it had such heroes and other forms of beautiful imageries, then it was certainly worth a try. Change the world and give bread to the poor? That was Christianity at its purest, and we were inspired.[48]

Or as another ELN member puts it:

> Although having denied religion, we the ELN were more religious than the same religions, more Christian than the same Christians; attempting to change a system for another that

---

45. Fidel expressed this frustration in 1968 when he stated, referring to the sectarianism of certain "revolutionary Latin America" organizations, "These are the paradoxes of history: when we see sectors of the clergy convert themselves into revolutionary forces, there are sectors of Marxism which become ecclesiastical forces" (Arenas, *La Guerrilla Por Dentro*, 101).

46. Hernández, "La Opción de los cristianos por la revolución," 48.

47. Correa, "Comentario," 96.

48. Author's interview, Joe Broderick, Bogotá, May 2011.

doesn't transcend death is to be condemned to repeat the cycle of our anguish . . .[49]

Camilo Torres' Death and His Iconography

In February 1966, only forty days after joining the ELN, Camilo Torres was killed in combat. He died "convinced in the duty to make the revolution as the only path toward a Christian fraternity of truth, in which the celebration of the Eucharist would acquire its true feeling."[50]

Prophetically, he had stated, "my death will open paths," and so it did, with masses of religious communities entering the ELN in that decade alone. He was able to link change with those alternative religious sectors with those struggles throughout Latin America.

> When this Catholic priest appeared [on the political stage], I became free of all sins, given that I come from a family that was on the one side Catholic and on the other revolutionary . . . A Catholic priest argued that a revolution was possible and that this was not a sin in the most Catholic country in Latin America, it was a great transformation.[51]

It is only when one understands how religion became so identified with the ELN's revolution, can one understand the interest awakened in the world for the figure of Camilo. As Broderick explains:

> What gives such significance to this history [of Camilo] is a factor which can only be called theological. And this in spite of the fact that Camilo was no theologian; he was a pastor—which is different. What happened was that his life, as he lived it, contained a lesson of ramifications practically biblical, and that was captured immediately—one doesn't know how—in the most diverse and remote places on the planet. The fact was that Camilo, spontaneously and without proposing it himself, became a Messiah . . . out of context.[52]

The early death of Camilo within the ELN in one of its first combat actions cloaked him in martyrdom, even sainthood. This beatification of Torres was and still is in keeping with the strong Catholic ethos of the

49. Correa, "Comentario," 93.
50. Broderick, Camilo, 16.
51. Zabala, "Comentario," 110.
52. Broderick, Camilo, 16.

ELN: one must die "in a state of grace" in combat actions to be placed on its altar of heroes. If you do not, and are shot for "unfaithfulness" without confession and penitence, you are condemned forever to "Hell."[53] This sense that one must die in order to be liberated is found in the ELN's own liturgical dates which commemorate the deaths of its combatants, particularly that of Camilo on February 15, which is practically a *dia de santo* (saint's day) within the ELN to this day.

But at the time of Camilo's entry into the ELN, *comandante* Fabio Vásquez tended to value Camilo more as a fund raiser for the movement. His disregard of Torres as a political strategist and leader of a populist movement in his own right is illustrated by Vásquez's willingness to allow him to go into combat despite his complete lack of training. Torres' political importance apparently did not become clear to the leadership until all the homages to Torres were made after his death, according to Jaime Arenas who wrote a critical book of the ELN before being assassinated by the ELN:

> The *jefe* of the ELN was not capable of understanding the political and strategic importance of Camilo . . . He had a myopic evaluation of Camilo, even his own political movement of masses for him was uncontrollable. For the *jefe* of the ELN, that populist surge had no [political] transcendence; it was only valued as an opportunity to obtain funds. The fact that millions of Colombians were on their feet listening to the revolutionary speeches of Camilo had only one possible importance for Fabio: the economic.[54]

53. One of the original founders, a combatant who was seen as "disloyal," condemned by an ELN council and shot by firing squad, was for many years erased from photos with Camilo Torres and the first leader Fabio Vásquez in the Cuban magazine *Bohemia*, in a Stalinist style of disappearance from history. This was rectified in the 1980s with a new, less sanctimonious ELN leadership and with the establishment of a *Frente Victor Medina Morón* in the department of César (Broderick, *El guerrillero invisible*, 37). Broderick argues that if Camilo had lasted within the ELN for several years, he probably would have been executed for questioning the leader's postulations, or for not "towing the line," or he would have abandoned the ELN, as quite a number did, at personal risk. This paranoia of the leadership was due principally to "the infantile form in which letters were written in pretend code which didn't exist," even for the ELN's own archives. These letters, passing between the urban and rural networks throughout the country, fell into the hands of the military intelligence and increased their knowledge of who, when and where—further escalating the leadership's paranoia and internal purges (Arenas, *La Guerrilla Por Dentro*, 121).

54. Arenas, *La Guerrilla Por Dentro*, 116–17. Arenas recognizes that one of the other serious concerns of Fabio Vasquez was that the Communist Party was "intel-

Thus, for Camilo Torres to be so seduced by the ELN and for his death to have such ramifications, indicates that a religious fervor is embodied in the very origins of the ELN and helps explain the attraction of so many people to the ELN "in a country which is so religious, so Catholic."[55]

The Epoch of Camilismo, Camilo Torres' Revolutionary Christianity

By introducing a vision of Revolutionary Christianity—a synthesis between Marxism and Christianity—Camilo provided a "theological and evangelical option of Christians for the revolution"—subsequently galvanizing an untold numbers of priests, nuns, seminarians, and Christians from the Christian Base Communities—"almost as a mass"—to join the ranks of the ELN. These included, in the late 1960s and 1970s, Franciscans, Jesuits, Claretians, members from the Community Marymount, as well as nonreligious members with links to bishops who did not belong to any particular religious community.[56] In one important case, in 1969, three Spanish priests—Manuel Pérez, Antonio Jimenez, and Domingo Laín—who had studied at the Mission Latin American Seminary in Madrid, arrived in Colombia, seeking to emulate the figure of Camilo.[57] Manuel Perez, although schooled in the Tridentine tradition of the Catholic Church, experienced, like Camilo, a period of enthusiasm for and then disillusionment with the traditional Catholic social doctrine focused primarily on breaking communist mobilizations. Despite serious and deadly difficulties with Fabio Vásquez, one of the original members of the Cuban Brigade, Manuel Pérez would come to lead the ELN in the 1980s, building its military capacity.

In one testimony, we learn of the ELN's appointed liaison person maintaining strong links with Christian communities, deacons and laymen and women who were committed to the ELN. These meetings led to organizing the first "Assembly Comandante Camilo Torres Restrepo" in 1986 which declared that for the Colombian revolution, it was essential to create an alliance between Christians and Marxists.[58] While

---

ligently advising [Camilo], surrounding him in a planned manner. Camilo's naivité and the skill [of the Communist Party] could create problems for us."

55. Broderick, *El guerrillero invisible*, 43. Author's interview with Broderick, Bogotá, 2011.

56. Hernández, "La Opción de los cristianos por la revolución," 58.

57. Ibid., 58.

58. This apparently was not news: this same declaration had been made by Fidel

there were long discussions about revolutionary Christianity, there were also discussions within different sectors of the ELN about the "type" of Marxism that should be practiced.

"There was a flourishing of radical Marxists, as within the Antioqueño sector of the ELN—*Columna Uno*—with its classic, orthodox Marxism which continued growing and developing within the ELN itself."[59]

In one book and interviews, we also learn of one nun's longterm commitment to the ELN for over twenty years, leaving her position as head of *Colegio Marymount* for young elite girls in Bogotá, to serve as its international representative in Central America in the 1980s. A lover of Fabio Vásquez, she had made a logistical error in which badly falsified identity papers had led to the capture of one militant. As a result, Vásquez ordered from Cuba that she be shot—an order refused by "Gabino,"[60] the leader of the ELN at the time.[61]

At this time, there was also an opening in the ELN for non-Catholic Christian sectors. Before this, the ELN had only been accepting Catholic priests, many of whom, upon their death, would have *frentes* named after them.[62] But with this new Assembly in 1986, a new kind of ecumenism emerged for those non-Catholics who opted for the armed struggle.

However, it is interesting to examine one *frente* for what it informs us about the contradictions that this new ecumenism raised for the ELN in attempting to combine Marxism with a variant of revolutionary Christianity.

Frente Domingo Laín emerged spontaneously in 1980 in the department of Arauca. It was formed by peasants who had earlier organized around social concerns and decided to join the armed struggle of the ELN. Previously, this *frente* had developed a dogmatic Marxism which had always fought against "the Christianity" within the ELN, and indeed had assassinated the Bishop of Arauca, Monsignor Jaramillo. The con-

---

Castro when he visited Salvador Allende in Chile, 1971 (Hernández, "Ponencia," 59).

59. Hernández, "La Opción de los cristianos por la revolución," 61.

60. His real name is Nicolás Rodriguez Bautista.

61. Calux Carriquiry, *La Búsqueda*; about Leonor Esguerra's life, author's interview in Bogotá, 2010; Ponsford, "Nuestra indignada. Entrevista con Leonor Esguerra Rojas"; "La monja guerrillera."

62. For example, El Frente Camilo Torres, el Frente Domingo Laín, la Regional Diego Cristobal Uribe, among others.

tradictions of this *frente* in some respects reflect the contradictions of the ELN itself. In the middle of the debate at the Assembly in 1986, this *frente* raised the question, "Why in a revolutionary organization which one supposes is Marxist and as such materialist, is there an idealistic priest as its head?" Hence, here is an ELN frente with a Catholic priest's name which objects to the Catholic priest leader, Manuel Perez—who himself did not wish to be addressed as "priest."

The Plus and Minus of Religion Within a Revolutionary Movement

Nevertheless, there was a plus and minus to ELN of this influx of the religious community. A plus was that it introduced a methodology which permitted the ELN, to a certain degree, in the midst of its crisis, to reconstruct its organization. Networks were rebuilt and communitarian work reengaged. One of the Spanish priests, Domingo Laín, had a great deal to do with this religious-political work, which was referred to as *replanteamiento* (reinstatement) in the 1970s. This coincided with two crises the ELN had to confront: desertions and internal executions by firing squad due to the authoritarian and paranoid attitude of ELN leader Fabio Vásquez as well as the defeat and killing of much of the Central Command (COCE) of the ELN by the Colombian military (at Anorí). At this point, Fabio Vásquez absconded to Cuba where he remains today.

The minus of this spontaneous influx of the religious community into the ELN ranks à la *camilismo* was a seeking after "a unity," a consensus: "We seek that which unites us and not that which separates us," according to Camilo Torres.[63] This consensus-building was essential for Manuel Pérez to be able to reconstruct and reinvigorate an entirely disparate ELN given the despair from the executions by firing squad and the use of violence rather than political debate. But in the long run, this seeking after consensus became itself a kind of straightjacket which impeded necessary political debates within the ELN.

> Because one felt at a certain moment when one confronted another with one's ideas, when one discussed them, shared points of view, that one was damaging this unity, this fraternity, that one was not in solidarity [with this consensus]. There was a negative ambience in regard to debate.[64]

63. Quoted in Hernández, "La Opción de los cristianos por la revolución," 60.
64. Ibid., 60.

The *camilismo*—the Marxist-Christian reflections—of the religious members within the ranks of the ELN, together with those militants on the outside committed to the ELN, to maintain "faith" in the revolutionary cause, and to *encarnarse* (to "sacrifice" one's life in the embodiment of a radical Christ), were linked up with the social-political urban work of the masses (el *Replanteamiento*)—very similar to how the *Frente Unido* networks of Torres and Arenas in the early days "saved" the ELN from extinction. Based on this alliance, it was able to vigorously strengthen its relations with communities, decentralize its hierarchy and expand into different parts of the country with revolutionary urban *frentes*.

Nonetheless, this strategic alliance between Marxism and Christianity was not without its difficulties. Sometimes one component would attempt to dominate the other without much success. At the Congress of the ELN in 1989, for example, leader Manuel Pérez suggested that every candidate to the *Dirección Nacional* agree to monogamy. "We told him that this was not a church and that the Catholic morality and the revolutionary ethic were two very different things."[65] The proposal was dropped.

Another Epoch of the ELN

In 1987, with more military capacity, a fusion was created between the ELN and the MIR-Patria Libre—a confluence of former Marxist-Leninist seminarians and other civilian urban mobilizations—with a name to concretely represent this fusion of "two humanisms: Marxist and Christian humanisms": *Unión Camilista-Ejército de Liberación Nacional* (UCELN). Such was the linkage made between the social movements and the ELN,[66] but the contradictions of Christian mysticism and Marxist military thinking still engendered a constant struggle to continually seek consensus.

With the fall of the Berlin Wall in 1989, there arose "political contradictions" with the leadership of Manuel Pérez and Nicolás Rodríguez Bautista ("Gabino"), differences in the way of interpreting this (new) international reality as well as with regard to the priorities given to political or military demands. The costs of this attempt of conform-to-consensus, together with the fall of the Wall, caused one major internal rupture in

65. Ibid., 65.
66. See Valencia, *Mis Años de Guerra*.

1991 for the ELN. *La Corriente de Renovación Socialista* (CRS), with over 1200 *elenos*, decided to initiate an internal political negotiation to exit from the ELN:

> with an emphasis on the debates, the circumstances and the form by which our return to civil society was to be constructed . . . The CRS gave up our arms based on a profound conviction of the end of the road for armed insurrection and the opening of the [new] 1991 Constitution as a partial pact of peace.[67]

As we've seen, early on, *elenos*, as both good Catholics and nationalists, rejected the more secular and international model provided by the traditional Communist Parties in the USSR, Cuba, and Colombia. But the irony is that it was the fall of the Berlin Wall and the clash of the more traditionally trained Christian mystics with those who were more open to civilian options, that led to this willingness on the part of some *elenos* to reject armed struggle and adopt a political model of struggle. This led to the major rupture.

Religion and Revolution: The Discourse of Sacrifice

In comparing the ideological discourse of the ELN as both a political and religious organization (as with many similar organizations of the Left in Latin America), one finds interesting convergences in the exercise of commitment and mission, or *entrega*.

As with strongly religious communities, for the ELN, the ample use of rhetoric and a recurrence to dialogue is seen as a necessary part of the elaboration of ideological concepts. But at the same time, this "dialogue" can also serve as "a mechanism by which to close the space . . . against other ways of thinking." It can be a reaffirmation of those concepts which "serve to sustain the vision which one has in the organization, its objectives, its commitment, before the world." Thus, anyone who may be opposed to the discourse itself "would be perceived as not only contradictory but as true enemies."[68]

As Arenas writes, the texts of the evangelical serve as the basis for this "theology of liberation in which the disciples of Jesus were in fact armed, and Jesus himself is a rebel, a revolutionary, an insurgent against the Roman Empire—a revolutionary ideology in its time. Although this

67. Cf. Célis, "Los protagonistas."
68. Brito, "El Fundamentalismo en la Política," 98–105.

history has been rewritten to make it more palatable, within the primitive fibre"[69] of Christianity, herein lies a radicalism that was taken up by militants both within and outside the ELN in Colombia. There are "claims that ELN documents exist which refer to this new species of radical Christianity through the establishment of new *frentes* of priests and nuns," but "it is unclear to what extent this religious fervor has been assimilated into the organization *per se*."[70]

If it is unclear the extent to which such radical Christian doctrine penetrated the ELN, there is one critical way in which Christian and ELN doctrine coincide. For both Christian radicals and *elenos*, there is a logic that argues that if one is willing to accede one's life, to give it up in the benefit of a cause, it remains equally so to demand of another that s/he give up hers/his: it authorizes and justifies the taking of the life of one's opponent. It validates the institutionalized use of violence. The role of martyr or redeemer is very similar in both contexts.

Open to a Peace Settlement?

Finally, one might ask whether the religious-consensual element has influenced the ELN to be open to peace and to end the armed struggle begun so fervently in Havana in 1963? This is not entirely clear. What is clear, though, is that of the insurgencies in Colombia, the ELN has been willing numerous times to seriously entertain the possibility of peace and to enter the realm of legitimate political action.[71] Father Camilo Torres's original ideas for the ecumenical Frente Unido plus revolutionary action still remain salient, as does his faith in making a better world through political action. As Leon Valencia, a CRS militant, argues,

> The greatest contribution that the [ELN] guerrillas could make to the development of the Left would be to move towards a peaceful resolution of the conflict. If peace negotiations should also provide an opportunity for reforms that strengthen democracy and address social needs in the regions, that contribution would

69. Arenas, *La Guerrilla Por Dentro*, 116–17.

70. Ibid.

71. The ELN participated in negotiations in 1991 with representatives of the government of Colombian President Gaviria in Caracas and Mexico, in 1997 in Madrid with President Samper's representatives, in 1998 in Germany and 2000 in Geneva and 2002 in Havana with President Pastrana's emissaries, and most recently, in 2006–2007 in Havana with President Uribe's Peace Commissioner.

be even greater. Putting an end to violence and bringing the war to a close would deprive the right of the pretexts it uses to justify its continued atrocities.[72] It is possible that the ELN has begun to understand this in the light of its own political traditions, based on the thinking of its principal leader, Father Camilo Torres Restrepo.[73]

SOME CONCLUDING REMARKS

How has religious belief served to construct within the ELN a justification for participating in the armed conflict in Colombia? Although the ELN is an insurgency that over time has identified itself with a particularly nationalist and ecumenical set of religious-political beliefs, this in no way makes the ELN a religious movement. It is true that of the two insurgent groups, it is the one in which religious concepts have played an important role in terms of ideological justifications for the use of force and as a way to distinguish itself from the FARC.[74]

Fervent religious belief appears to have remained rather peripheral to the ELN's military and political vision yet visibly central to its identity as a movement in which so many Catholic priests, nuns, and seminarians have participated.[75] Hence, while one could say that the icon of sacrifice and *entrega* that for Father Camilo Torres served as an impulse to mobilize militants from various religious orders, and that at times

72. Kidnapping has been the major source of revenue for the ELN over the years. At negotiations in Germany in 1998, the ELN "stated very frankly—or, in the opinion of some attendees, with shocking audacity—that it would give up kidnapping only if another source of financing could be found through the peace process . . . This discussion was left open, but the ELN took the symbolic step of signing an agreement stating that it would not kidnap pregnant women or anyone over 75 years of age. This agreement unleashed a controversy in Colombia, with critics saying that the signatories of the document tacitly accepted the kidnapping of individuals who did not fall into either of the two exempt categories" (Valencia, "The ELN's Halting Moves toward Peace in Colombia," 107).

73. Valencia, "The ELN's Halting Moves toward Peace in Colombia," 107.

74. See Patiño, *Las Verdaderas Intenciones de las FARC* and *Guerras Inútiles*; cf. Medina and Ramón, *El Orden de la Guerra.*

75. See Molly Duft Toft's distinction between those conflicts in which combatants were fighting over whether a state or religion should be ruled according to a specific religion as central to their struggle, or where they identified with a specific religious tradition and grouped themselves accordingly, but where the rule of a specific religious tradition could not be considered the object of their contention, as cited in Mantilla, "What is the Link between Religion and Violence?," 28.

of crisis saved the movement from having to be dissolved as a guerrilla organization, the ELN cannot be characterized by reference to religious belief alone; nor has it ever been self-consciously a religious movement.[76] This notwithstanding, to understand an insurgency in which religion has played an important, if ambivalent, role is in itself worthy. It is important if, for no other reason, it allows us to see an insurgency as a complex movement full of contradictions and internal struggles both practical and doctrinal. If the ELN owes much of its growth and importance to its involvement with so many whose religious beliefs were central to their reasons for joining, it still remains unclear how dominant religion was in shaping the strategic realities on the ground. It also shows us that doctrinal justification can use parallel logics to justify violence—be they religious or secular. Finally, it suggests that religious beliefs, whether dominant or not, have influenced the overall thinking of an insurgency that owes so much of its following to a religious fervor for social justice.

What is clear is that the original seeking of grace by the ELN and by Father Torres—by way of both reason and faith—remains unresolved through revolutionary means.

BIBLIOGRAPHY

Arenas Reyes, Jaime. *La Guerrilla Por Dentro*. Bogotá: Ediciones Tercer Mundo, 2009.

Brito, Fernando. "El Fundamentalismo en la Politica, Elementos de Analisis." In *Las Verdaderas Intenciones del ELN*, edited by Corporacion Observatorio para la Paz, 98–105. Bogotá: Intermedio, 2001.

Broderick, Walter J. *Camilo: El Cura Guerrillero*. Bogotá: Intermedio, 2005.

———. *El guerrillero invisible*. Bogotá: Intermedio, 2000.

———. "Ponencia: La búsqueda de una iglesia distinta." In *Las Verdaderas Intenciones del ELN*, edited by Corporación Observatorio para la Paz, 28–44. Bogotá: Intermedio, 2001.

———. "Revolución o Revolcón?" In *El regreso de los rebeldes: De la furia de las armas a los pactos, la crítica y la esperanza*, edited by Leon Valencia et al., 99–122. Bogotá: Corporacion Nuevo Arco Iris y CAREC, 2005.

Burgos, Élizabeth "L'Operation Pedro Pan: la rèvolution cubaine et l'instrumentalisation de l'enfance dans le cadre d'une guerre civile (1959–1962)." In *Entre mémoire collective et histoire officielle. L'histoire du temps présent en Amérique latine*, edited by Luc Capdevila and Frédérique Langue, 27–52. Rennes, France: Presses Universitaires de Rennes, 2009.

Calux Carriquiry, Inés. *La Búsqueda: Testimonio de Leonor Esguerra Rojas*. Medellín: Pregón, 2011.

76. See Giovanni Mantilla's overview of the literature on conflict and religion "What is the Link between Religion and Violence?," 25–41.

Célis, Luis Eduardo. "Los protagonistas, los hechos y los tiempos. Cronologia y cronica." In *El regreso de los rebeldes. De la furia de las armas a los pactos, la crítica y la esperanza*, edited by Leon Valencia et al., 123–43. Bogotá: Corporación Nuevo Arco Iris y CAREC, 2005.

Correa, Medardo. "Comentario: Sobre mi Vivencia en el Eln." In *Las Verdaderas Intenciones del ELN*, edited by Corporacion Observatorio para la Paz, 88–195. Bogotá: Intermedio, 2001.

"Exterminio al ELN." In *Cambio*, February 5–11, 2007.

"FARC contra ELN. Las FARC quieren aniquilar al ELN su intención de llegar a un acuerdo de paz con el gobierno." In *Semana*, 5 de febrero, 2007.

Hernández Valencia, Fernando. "La búsqueda del socialismo democratic." In *El regreso de los rebeldes. De la furia de las armas a los pactos, la crítica y la esperanza*, edited by Leon Valencia et al., 121–67. Bogotá: Corporación Nuevo Arco Iris y CAREC, 2005.

———. "Ponencia: La Opción de los Cristianos por la Revolución." In *Las Verdaderas Intenciones del ELN*, edited by Corporación Observatorio para la Paz, 48–66. Bogotá: Intermedio, 2001.

Mantilla, Giovanni. "What Is the Link between Religion and Violence?" *Análisis Político* 70 (September–December 2010) 25–41.

Medina Ferro, Juan Guillermo, and Graciela Uribe Ramón. *El Orden de la Guerra: LAS FARC-EP: Entre la organización y la política*. Bogotá: Centro Editorial Javeriana, 2002.

Molano Bravo, Alfredo "Trochas y fusiles: Historias de combatientes." Bogotá: El Ancora, 2007.

"La monja guerrillera." In *Semana*, September 19, 2011.

Patiño, Otty. *Las Verdaderas Intenciones de las FARC*. Bogotá: Intermedio, 1999.

———. *Guerras Inutiles, Corporacion Observatorio para la Paz*. Bogotá: Intermedio, 2009.

Ponsford, Marianne. "Nuestra indignada: Entrevista con Leonor Esguerra Rojas." *Revista Arcadia*, September 2011.

Sharpless, Richard E. *Gaitán of Colombia: A Political Biography*. Pittsburgh: University of Pittsburgh Press, 1978.

Valencia Agudelo, León. "The ELN's Halting Moves toward Peace in Colombia." In *Columbia: Building Peace in a Time of War*, edited by Virginia M. Bouvier, 95–109. Washington DC: United States Institute of Peace, 2009.

———. *Mis Años de Guerra*. Bogotá: Corporación Nuevo Arco Iris, 2008.

Vargas Velasquez, Alejo. "Anotaciones sobre el discurso ideólogico y político del ELN." In *Las Verdaderas Intenciones del ELN*, edited by Corporacion Observatorio para la Paz, 72–83. Bogotá: Intermedio, 2001.

Zabala, Vladimir. "Comentario: Marxismo y Cristianismo en el ELN." In *Las Verdaderas Intenciones del ELN*, edited by Corporacion Observatorio para la Paz, 106–13. Bogotá: Intermedio, 2001.

6

Religion, Conflict, and Peace-Building

The Case of Sri Lanka

MARIYAHL HOOLE, NARI SENANAYAKE, *and* JEHAN PERERA

In an address to parliament on May 19, 2009, Sri Lanka's President, Mahinda Rajapaksa announced the end of Asia's longest running civil war. As he noted in his nationally televised address, for the first time in almost three decades "the writ of the state now runs across every inch of . . . territory . . . we have completely defeated terrorism."[1] However, the military defeat of the Liberation Tigers of Tamil Eelam (LTTE) only eliminated a symptom of a much more pervasive and resilient disease. There is a broad consensus among historians and political scientists that the fundamental grievances of ethnic minorities predate the outbreak of armed conflict in 1983.[2] Furthermore, the experience of twenty-six years of civil war, in itself, has created new grievances and challenges which persist in spite of the government's recent military victory. In particular, state–minority relations continue to be defined by the conflict dynamics of the past.

The overwhelming tendency in the literature on Sri Lanka is to label the conflict as "ethnic."[3] The cultural diversity found in Sri Lanka is

1. Rajapaksa, "Address by HE President Mahinda Rajapaksa."

2. Bush, *The Intra-Group Dimensions of Ethnic Conflict in Sri Lanka*; De Silva, *Reaping the Whirlwind*; DeVotta, "Control Democracy, Institutional Decay, and the Quest for Eelam"; Imtiyaz, "Ethno-Political Conflict in Sri Lanka"; Manoharan, *Democratic Dilemma*; Peebles, *The History of Sri Lanka*.

3. Imtiyaz and Stavis, "Ethno-Political Conflict in Sri Lanka," 135; Peleg, *Democratising the Hegemonic State*, 3–6; Sabaratnam, *Ethnic Attachments in Sri Lanka*; DeVotta, "Control Democracy, Institutional Decay, and the Quest for *Eelam*," 66; Bush,

undeniably an essential dimension of this conflict. The majority, at about 75 percent of the population, is Sinhalese. The rest is divided among the Sri Lankan Tamils (11.4 percent), who compete with the Sinhalese for claims of historical entitlement to the land; the Sri Lankan Moors (8.2 percent), who trace their roots to Arab traders; and the Indian Tamils (5.0 percent), who were brought to the island as plantation workers by the British.[4] However, it is important to note that ethnicity is one of multiple axes of identity and its importance in conflict varies over time. In an effort to refine the prevalent discourse on Sri Lanka's conflict, this chapter examines how religious identity is connected to the outbreak of "ethnic" conflict.

Since the late nineteenth century, there have been increasing instances of religious intolerance and conflict in Sri Lanka. In the post-Independence period, this trend has intensified. The Sinhalese have been very effectively mobilized through Buddhism; similarly Tamil-speaking Muslims assert a more distinct identify for themselves based on their religion. Hinduism, another early religion of Sri Lanka, is associated with having "purer" Tamil roots. The one exception in the Sri Lankan case is the small Christian population, which is less reliant on ethnic markers as its membership includes both Sinhalese and Tamils. These interactions between ethnicity and religion suggest that even though race is the primary source of social stratification in Sri Lanka, people are always "aware of the religious identities associated with different communities"[5] and that all religions have political elements to them.

The mobilization of religious identities plays a key role in the war's social and political history. To maintain power, the traditional Sinhala elite politicised Sinhala-Buddhist identity and drew upon religio-cultural symbolism to unite the Sinhala-Buddhists into a base of electoral support. In doing so, the political elite ignored the needs of Sri Lanka's minorities, severely damaging its relations with them. In response to the increasing Sinhala-Buddhist dominance of political structures, Sri Lankan Tamils began to harden their own ethnic boundaries, eventually giving rise to a volatile form of Tamil nationalism around which the rebel group, the LTTE, was organised. Meanwhile, Tamil-speaking Muslims began to assert their own distinct ethnic identity, fearing that

---

The Intra-Group Dimensions of Ethnic Conflict in Sri Lanka.

4. *Population by Ethnicity, Census Years.*

5. Flanigan, "Faith and Fear in Development."

their particular sociopolitical and economic interests would be marginalized in a broader Tamil-speaking coalition. This intertwining of ethnicity and religion means that the "ethnic" conflict also occupies a religious dimension. A potent attack on Sinhala identity, for example, was the bombing of the *Dalada Maligawa* Temple, which houses the venerated tooth of the Buddha. Meanwhile, under an ethnic cleansing program in the Northern Province, the LTTE forcibly expelled its entire Muslim population so it could create a mono-ethnic Tamil state.

The politicization of religion has also become a major impediment to peace-building in Sri Lanka. The history of religious interference in political and social peace-building has impacted negatively on the potential of religions to advocate for reconciliation and forge peace. Furthermore, the recent political regime, one that invested all its energy and resources in a military "solution," is reluctant to reconcile with minority groups through a political reform process that emphasises democratic values, the rule of law, and human rights. Current faith-based, peace-building efforts cannot be removed from this history or context.

In spite of these challenges, religious organisations are theoretically well-equipped to mitigate divisions and promote peace. It is important to emphasize that identity is fluid and dynamic; it is not fixed and immutable. As such, influential leaders and faith-based organizations have the power to shift identities towards a position that is more closely aligned with religious ideals of virtue. Interreligious cooperation and dialogue could potentially promote this change. This paper, therefore, also analyses the strengths and weaknesses of recent religious efforts which attempt to bridge divides and encourage compassionate crosscultural relations at all levels of society. These initiatives provide hope that religious identity may, in time, become a force of change more than continuity.

OBSTACLES TO FAITH-BASED PEACE-BUILDING

The concept of religion, especially that of a "patriotic" religion that is linked to history, can provide many barriers to an effective negotiation of peace. While its fundamental nature is one of human faith, religion is also an intricate binding of social, political, and moral mores. These mores form a core attribute of both individual and group identity, even when these are opposed to typical social norms. In times of politicized cultural contentions, such as those being battled in Sri Lanka even today, this religious identity is strengthened and mobilized, allowing it to hold significant influence over how intercultural relationships take place.[6]

The primary effect of such mobilization is to affirm group boundaries and to protect group interests.[7] Since the character of religion persuades the group of moral superiority, it becomes vital that the values and beliefs of the groups, and indeed the very existence of the group, are defended. As Tessa Bartholomeusz has observed, "religious thinking, be it Jewish, Christian, Muslim, Hindu, or Buddhist, that takes seriously the relationship of ethics, morality and power, contains just-war thought."[8] This means that a religious group allows itself to engage in conflict when it is internally justified, even when such conflict seems inconsistent with its simultaneous messages of peace and goodwill.

Reconciling these two seemingly divergent results of religious belief has been a source of much intellectual and social debate. It is clear, however, that using religious rhetoric in times of cultural conflict can create an energetic nexus of group power. Such religious mobilization, although not the direct cause of the Sri Lankan conflict, has undeniably bolstered the tensions that compelled the war. Sri Lankan history is scattered with many instances where religious and ethnic concerns interacted to prevent peace. For example, one of the earliest negotiations between the Sinhala dominated government and the Tamil political parties (the Bandaranaike-Chelvanayakam Pact, 1957) was abrogated when Buddhist monks organized a protest on the prime minister's front lawn.[9] Today, we still see peace combated on religious grounds, such as when peace-building NGOs and individuals are painted as vehicles for Christian subversion, and are thus perceived to endanger the survival of the nation's ancient cultures.

This conflation of religious and ethnic identity has been a crucial dimension in Sri Lanka's civil war. Historical myths and narratives have been used to construct ideological justifications for Sinhala-Buddhist dominance. The sixth-century chronicle, *Mahavamsa*, for instance, is heavily influenced by the view of the Buddhist clergy as protectors of

6. Wellman and Tokuno, "Is Religious Violence Inevitable?," 292.

7. Ibid., 291.

8. Bartholomeusz, "In Defense of Dharma," 3.

9. For a detailed discussion of the *Bandaranaike-Chelvanayagam Pact* see: DeVotta, "From Ethnic Outbidding to Ethnic Conflict"; De Silva, "Regionalism and Decentralisation of Power."

Buddhism and "the island of Sri Lanka as the Buddhist Promised Land."[10] Since the country is construed as the sacred stronghold of Buddhism, it becomes vital that it is protected from conquest or adulteration. In the early post-independence era, sections of the Sinhalese political elite employed this notion of a sacrosanct Sinhala-Buddhist heritage to unite and mobilise the Sinhala people; unfortunately, however, such politics also served to increase the country's ethnic divisions and precipitate its civil war. Furthermore, these historical myths have created a milieu that justifies the ascendancy and dominance of the political class and Buddhist establishment. This is manifest in the ongoing election of some sections of the Buddhist clergy to the parliament.[11] Their campaign platform emphasizes Sinhala-Buddhist supremacy and a strong commitment to a centralised, unitary governmental structure. Although a centralized government would allow them to continue in their historical roles as political advisors, this vision jars with that of the nation's minorities, who would prefer to see a federal system of devolved government in which their own interests can be realized.

The connections between ethnicity and religion in the Sri Lankan Tamil community are more complex. The LTTE, at least publicly, repudiated caste-based stratification, and as such, it was not always in its interests to incorporate the "traditional" Tamil heritage of Hinduism in its nationalistic rhetoric. Occasionally, however, the Hindu identity of the Tamils is utilized to speak out against the group's enemies—for instance, Muslims, on both ethnic and religious grounds, are excluded from the Tamil category,[12] while Christians who disagree with the ideals of Tamil nationalism are sometimes targeted through their religion. Indeed, in many regards, Tamil Hindus have used their religious traditions to "energize and mobilise their cultural and political action against the dominant political structures" with continuing belief in an ancient heritage that lies in its connection to the *ur*, or land.[13]

---

10. Bartholomeusz, "In Defense of Dharma," 20.

11. Many monks contest in elections as part of the *Jathika Hela Urumaya* (National Heritage Party).

12. This is also tied to Muslim self-determination.

13. Juergensmeyer, quoted in Wellman and Tokuno, "Is Religious Violence Inevitable?," 292.

Since both Sinhalese and Tamils feel that their existence is threatened,[14] a large majority perceived the nationalistic conflict as a necessary evil. In the current climate of Sinhala-Buddhist triumphalism and continued ethnic tension, it also becomes dangerous for members of either group to speak of a peaceful reconciliation. Since peace necessitates negotiating with those perceived as the "enemy" and maintaining a sustained collaboration, it is construed as diametrically opposed to the values of ethnic patriotism. Those who work for peace are thus branded as traitors, and are publicly vilified as such.

Since religion has been so effectively conflated with the conflict, it becomes particularly difficult for religious leaders to abandon the norm and speak for peace. As representatives of their group's beliefs their public personas are subject to both external and internal pressure. Precisely because the Buddhist establishment has a vested interest in the status quo it is extremely difficult for monks to openly support a political peace. Accordingly, the current trend among many eminent Buddhist monks is to support their nationalist ideology of the Sinhala dominated government and view Sri Lanka's complex conflict as a "war on terror."

The religious dimensions of conflict in Sri Lanka have also recently assumed a Buddhist-Christian dynamic, which renders it even more difficult for religious leaders to engage in interreligious peace programmes. In recent years, Sri Lankan Christians have been accused of using dishonorable methods to persuade Buddhists and Hindus away from their traditional religious heritage.[15] Evangelical Christians, who aim to convert, are perceived as particularly dangerous in Sri Lanka, and are even targeted by Christians of other denominations.[16] Since religion is so central to ethnic identity in Sri Lanka, it is easy to understand why the proselytizing themes of this "foreign" religion have inspired fear and suspicion. Sri Lankan Christians have thus been at the receiving end of frequent violence, and was the motivating factor behind the proposed

14. The Sinhalese, though a majority in the nation, feel threatened by the large population of Tamils who surround them in the region. This "minority complex" of the Sinhalese is theorized to contribute to their need for political power. De Silva, *A History of Sri Lanka*, 513.

15. This is largely due to the fact that humanitarian organizations (which are often seen as tools of Western imperialism) often have some Christian affiliations through leadership or employees.

16. Flanigan, "Faith and Fear in Development," 8.

Anti-Conversion Law of 2005, which reemerged in an amended form in 2009.

The perceived "threat" of Christian conversions may impede the peace-building potential of the cross-ethnic and crosscultural bonds *within* the Christian community in Sri Lanka. Those outside the group may fear that continuing interaction with the Christians could escalate conversions, while the Christians themselves may be put off by previous levels of aggression. It is important to recognise that such insecurity could become a major obstacle to peace-making, since it fosters nationalism and can be found in all four of Sri Lanka's major religions. The Buddhists are afraid that the honor and privileges accorded to their religion will subside. The Hindus, who are predominantly Tamil, are aware of their precarious place in Sri Lanka, and could benefit by supporting the Tamil separatist call. Meanwhile, the Muslims have particular reason to be cautious, often being crushed in the middle with little political power. Such apprehension is difficult to contest, since religious groups in Sri Lanka remain fairly isolated at the grassroots level. They often choose to interact within their own religions circles, and even display high levels of residential segregation. This means that these fears remain very much alive, and manifest themselves at times of great stress, such as when Sinhala-Buddhists attacked the Muslims in Mawanella in 2005, or when the LTTE killed over thirty Buddhist monks in the East in 1985.

It is important to keep these fears in mind when trying to establish an interreligious effort for peace. Those organizing such a project must understand that each religious group has its own specific concerns, and that forming a unified idea of "peace" will be a difficult task. It must also be understood that while there may be some level of consensus among the leaders, this may not immediately be translated to the public. Competing nationalisms and exclusivist group identities will be the hardest to combat. Religion is crucial to the Buddhist majority since it justifies their claim to political supremacy; for the nation's minorities, it is even more precious since it provides "experiences of transcendent power and socialisation that protects them from out group exposure."[17]

Warfare that operates on religious lines is a powerful means of boundary formation. By linking ethnic objectives to sacred pasts, Sinhalese, Tamils, and Muslims have been able to activate and sustain the powerful divisions between them. While religion can be used to

17. Wellman and Tokuno, "Is Religious Violence Inevitable?," 294.

strengthen such boundaries, however, it also carries the potential to break ethnic divides and facilitate humanitarianism and peace. Religions usually advocate similar messages of love, benevolence, and spiritual development. Many believe that the parallels between their ideals could be used to motivate "a common religious language of conciliation that can foster a genuine spirit of forgiveness and reconciliation."[18]

FAITH BASED PEACE-BUILDING EFFORTS IN SRI LANKA

There are currently a number of different religious and interreligious efforts that are attempting to create and promote peace in Sri Lanka. Their work ranges from development projects to humanitarian aid. Faith-based efforts hold immense potential to create peace in Sri Lanka. With the moral authority to decry conflict, and the social networks to mobilize support and public action, religious groups could spread the message of peace in effective and sustainable ways. In particular, interreligious initiatives which aim to bridge ethno-religious divides and establish a discourse of understanding (even in the face of severe opposition), provide hope that a desire for peace is still alive.

Literature in the field of religious peacemaking identifies a number of specific, though not unique, strengths which faith-based actors possess. These include "strong faith-based motivation, long-term commitment, long-term presence on the ground, moral and spiritual authority, and a niche to mobilise others for peace."[19] Religious interventions can take many forms, involving local religious bodies, grassroots initiatives, or actions by religious leaders to bridge "the divide between faiths, to engage in dialogue, build relationships, and develop trust and work together to resolve common problems."[20] One particular asset of faith-based peace-building in Sri Lanka is that most people in the country are oriented towards their own religious community; thus when these interventions are framed by religious narratives and contexts, they become much more effective in persuading involved parties towards peace.

Religious peace-building in Sri Lanka is organised at two different levels. The interreligious councils headed by leaders of national religious organisations, hold interventions and publicly speak for humanitarian-

---

18. Johnston, "The Religious Dimensions of Peacebuilding," 8.

19. Bouta, Kadayifci-Orellana, and Abu-Nimer. *Faith-Based Peace-Building*, 8.

20. Johnston, "The Religious Dimensions," 8.

ism and peace. Meanwhile, there are less publicized efforts at the grass-roots which are also powerful advocates for a sustainable peace.

INSTITUTIONAL INTERRELIGIOUS EFFORTS

Institutional faith-based peace-building efforts in Sri Lanka aim to harness the influence and action of prominent members of all religious communities. This is not an easy task given the afore mentioned obstacles. However, religious leaders also operate with distinct advantages when it comes to faith-based conflict resolution and peace-building. Indeed, Sri Lanka's religious leadership has access to several critical resources that could assist peace-building initiatives in Sri Lanka. The extensive, well-established religious networks and institutions in Sri Lanka are valuable channels of communication and action. In fact, religious leaders generally have extensive reach and influence in Sri Lankan society, as the majority of the population belongs to a religious community, and are thus accessible through religious infrastructure. Furthermore, these religious leaders occupy crucial intermediary roles in Sri Lankan society. In the period immediately prior to the commencement of the Norwegian facilitated peace process in 2002, for example, Christian bishops acted as facilitators carrying messages between the leadership of the Sri Lankan government and leaders of the LTTE.

It is also important to note that their leadership is constant and durable, especially when contrasted with the country's political leaders who are vulnerable to the pressures of a democratic electorate, and thus change more frequently. Indigenous religious leaders are long-term players, who have been present throughout the lengthy lifecycle of Sri Lanka's conflict. As a result, they are well poised to provide much needed continuity in approaches and commitment to peace-building initiatives and advocacy in Sri Lanka. The religious clergy maintains a very close relationship with the people of the country. Thus, they are well situated to undertake observatory and educational roles to discourage violence, corruption, human rights violations or other behavior which impedes viable and sustainable peace-building initiatives. If Sri Lanka's top religious leaders were to unite in favor of a common cause, it would be difficult for any government, political party, or rebel group to put forward its own agenda against them.

In Sri Lanka religious leaders (especially Buddhist monks) can be particularly influential in political decision-making processes due to the status and respect they hold in Sri Lankan society and their close links with the political establishment.[21] This ability to influence politicians is a critical resource which can be drawn upon to initiate the political and constitutional changes necessary for a sustainable solution to Sri Lanka's conflict. Additionally, Sri Lanka's religions are organised at local, national and international levels, and thus are a vital link to global resources and encouragement. Religious leaders thus possess the capability to mobilise widespread support for a peace process.[22] International support for peace could be a potential defense against the strong opposition of nationalist parties which discourages many religious leaders from taking up the cause. On the other hand, such international involvement may lead to perceptions of foreign interference and deter indigenous efforts.

In light of the failure of successive governments to find a political solution to the Sri Lankan conflict, many civic and religious organisations have attempted to mobilise religious leaders in support of a sustainable social and political change. Multireligious peace initiatives such as the Congress of Religious and the Sri Lanka Council of Religions for Peace not only merge the strengths of the four Sri Lankan religions into one collective power, but demonstrate first hand that unity and concord between groups is possible. Bishop Vianney Fernando of the Roman Catholic Church, believed that this was the most valuable aspect of these inter-religious organisations, as witnessing harmony between their spiritual leaders holds powerful influence over the Sri Lankan people.[23] At a time when the political leadership has failed to substantially alter the status quo, strong interreligious initiatives at the top level could become a very persuasive argument for peaceful dialogue and reconciliation.

The Congress of Religions (CoR)

At the institutional level, the Congress of Religions is perhaps the most prominent of all exclusively interfaith efforts to date. An organization that enjoys the membership of powerful leaders from all four faiths, the Congress convenes periodically to issue statements on national concerns such as violence at elections and matters of good governance. It

21. Orjuela, *Civil Society in Civil War*, 181–82.

22. Johnston, "The Religious Dimensions of Peacebuilding," 55.

23. Interview with Bishop V. Fernando, November 23, 2008.

has also used its influence to lobby the Sri Lankan political leadership and express its opposition to violence and injustice.

The Congress has increased its activities by forming a select delegation of Goodwill Ambassadors who, if they can maintain their commitment to these intensive roles, could become very effective advocates for the people. Their significant standing in social and political circles means that these ambassadors have access to sensitive information. Their first tour of Sri Lanka, for instance, included visits to Internally Displaced Peoples (IDP) camps in the conflict hardened areas of Batticaloa and Vavuniya; a Military Hospital on the brink of the conflict zone; and a meeting with the Commander-in-Chief of Vavuniya in the Army Headquarters, all of which were barred to other actors. More recently when the government-appointed Lessons Learnt and Reconciliation Commission (LLRC) came out with its final report in November 2011, the Congress of Religions issued a strong statement in support of the LLRC report.[24] The LLRC report is an official and public document as it investigates and analyzes the causes of conflict and problems of governance in the country and suggests remedies to these problems. It has been strongly criticized by Tamil political parties and international human rights groups as favoring the government and downplaying civilian deaths. It has also been commended by national civil society groups and sections of the international community as providing a basis for political reform. The Congress of Religions called on civil society to be active in taking this message to the grassroots through an awareness creation and advocacy campaign.

The Sri Lanka Council of Religions for Peace (SLCRP)

The Sri Lanka Council of Religions for Peace (which grew out of the National Conference on Religion and Peace) is the local body of the international interreligious organization, Religions for Peace (formerly known as The World Conference of Religions for Peace). The SLCRP has many means of influence; the religious leaders who form its membership are prominent figures who are active in both politics and society, it receives substantial funding from its international patron, and is promoted by influential civil society actors. In contrast to the Congress, which focuses more on the societal effects of war, SLCRP has as one of

---

24. The LLRC Report highlighted the lessons learned from the period of war.

its objectives to directly address the politics of Sri Lanka's conflict. This includes engaging in activities to transform the values of the political leadership, civil society, and its own politicized spiritual body towards a harmonious peace, while involving itself in multilevel diplomacy to encourage reconciliation between the country's ethnic groups.

Much of the SLCRP's work in recent times has focused on national and district conferences which bring together both the religious elite and the local religious leaders. In November 2008, SLCRP members joined delegates from Religions for Peace, local religious leaders, and their partner organisation, the National Peace Council, in a conference addressing the humanitarian crisis taking place in the North. SLCRP members spoke of the need for a humanitarian corridor to allow trapped civilians to escape the conflict zone, and the conference ended with the discussion and ratification of a statement that urged such a corridor. Along with the international delegates, the SLCRP presented this statement to the President of Sri Lanka.

SLCRP has also engaged in some grassroots work, building rain-fed water tanks for Hindu, Buddhist and Muslim communities in border districts as a symbol of interethnic and interreligious harmony. However, after 2009 the primarily Buddhist leadership of the SLCRP decided to delink itself from other NGOs and work on its own. This was on account of its concerns that peace NGOs were discredited and being targeted as unpatriotic by nationalist groups, which was a label that the SLCRP did not wish to see attached to itself. It also decided to steer away from taking any actions or issue statements that could be construed as being critical of the government in a post-war context in which Sinhalese nationalism was being stoked by the government. Instead it looks to develop district committees with a focus on local humanitarian issues in order to build up local interreligious councils and strengthen interreligious relationships at the ground level.

Inter-Religious Peace Foundation (IRPF)

Initiated when the National Christian Council recognized the benefits of multifaith collaboration, the Inter-Religious Peace Foundation was created with the purpose of bringing together the diverse powers of the four religions into one effective task force for peace. The IRPF is built on past relationships between religious leaders. Since it is founded on the idea of interreligious cooperation and solidarity, the IRPF is unique in how it shares power: whereas other interfaith peace organizations have delegated leadership to key Buddhist monks (since they hold the most political and social leverage), the IRPF chairpersonship is rotated so that all religions are equally represented. The chairpersonship is also a joint privilege, shared between two religions at any given time.

The primary goal of IRPF is to utilize the different strengths of each religion to speak for good governance, help the people, and to advocate for peace. During the cease-fire, the IRPF sent its members to talk to the LTTE and the Government, trying to persuade each side to begin the necessary action to forge a united peace. They also were involved in activism and peace-building during the war, including advocacy against the use of landmines.

The key strength of the IRPF, however, is its work with the people. In the past, the IRPF has been involved in a range of activities, from helping displaced populations resettle in new communities, to providing food and other humanitarian assistance to those caught in refugee camps. It particularly concerns itself with victims of violence and the poor, directing the material resources of each religious community towards their assistance. Believing that "religiosity can act as a unifying factor among individuals and communities of different religious and ethnic backgrounds,"[25] all activities of the IRPF are targeted towards building peace through encouraging interethnic harmony. However, at the present time the organization has not been able to maintain its previous level of work.

Grassroots Movements for Peace

Collaborative efforts between top religious leaders, like the ones detailed above, are powerful since they hold influence over the political sphere and have easy access to the public eye. However, as of yet, these organizations have not had a holistic impact on Sri Lankan society since they have not been able to branch out into extensive, effective grassroots work. One cannot underestimate the importance of work at the community level in a country where decades of propaganda and the fear and suspicion generated by war, have had a formidable impact.

Those organizations which attempt to work at the grassroots level often find that progress is discouragingly slow. It is widely believed that

25. Bilodeau, *The Inter-Religious Peace Foundation*, 17.

the people are politically apathetic and are too afraid of retribution to be involved in political affairs. This is a justifiable concern; however, it must also be remembered that much of the population remains in a state of poverty and does not have the opportunity to think about ideological issues when their very survival is so difficult to pursue. Furthermore, they have become subject to the nationalist propaganda regularly circulated by the media (especially media which is state-owned). Seminars, pamphlets and other educational materials, though they may be useful, will thus have limited impact at the grassroots level.

Peace work at the grassroots must, therefore, include a means of empowering the people and improving their lives. While the institutional peace organizations recognize this in their attempts to address specific needs of the people, an organization that has taken this precept further is The Sarvodaya Sharamadana Movement. Working intensively at the grassroots level, Sarvodaya believes in "peace through development," and uses the concept of a common human spirituality to heal hostile relations and create and community-based solidarity.

Although infused with Buddhist values, Sarvodaya works through a crosscultural, interreligious attempt at bottom-up peace-building. Since it views peace as one of many human needs, it organizes programs in which peace and village-level development goes hand in hand. During these programs, people from many religions and ethnic backgrounds convene to work on a common project—building a road or clearing a local field, for example—that both enhances their community, and builds strong human ties. Since people overlook barriers such as race, religion or political affiliation to solve a mutual problem, it establishes a sense of a common humanity and allows for an empathetic understanding of the other to take place.

Sarvodaya's work highlights the positive effects of a grassroots movement for peace. Working in more than 15,000 villages all across the country (including the war-stricken Northeast), Sarvodaya has been able to persuade both the people and their immediate leaders to support and maintain an active peace. Since it recognizes that a holistic effort is needed for full peace to occur, Sarvodaya also works at the district, zonal, and national levels; however, it is most recognized for its advances at the grassroots.

Another organization that has sought to work with religious clergy to achieve peace-building outcomes and reconciliation is the National

Peace Council. NPC started a project to promote cooperation among multi-religious communities in Sri Lanka, focusing on groups who have been divided by the conflict. Accordingly in each target area, a District-level Inter-Religious Council (DIRC) was established and strengthened in close cooperation with the District Action Committees (DACs).

The overall objective of the NPC is to create peaceful relations between all communities in Sri Lanka's diverse population contributing to a healing society in a post-war context. The intention is to promote multireligious community responsiveness of groups who have been divided by the conflict and enable them to find appropriate humanitarian solutions to care for conflict-affected women and children.

DIRCs, which are active in twelve districts, have direct access to grassroots communities, enabling them to understand and voice their concerns. The committee members have contacts with higher-level religious leaders and those with political command, and are in a position to inform and influence them. By having a structure so closely tied to a grassroots organizing structure, NPC has been able to empower local CBO leaders and maintain a bottom up approach in finding solutions to humanitarian needs through a multireligious perspective.

DIRCs have two primary roles in furthering peace at the grassroots. One is offering local religious communities opportunities to undertake multi-religious action and advocacy for peace, while their second objective is to help local communities create a strong internal solidarity regardless of ethnic or religious division. At the community level, the DIRCs mediate in local conflicts between ethnic or religious groups, easing the tension and suspicion that is residual from the war. Being leaders from the communities in which they mediate, DIRCs are attuned to the local dynamics of a larger national conflict, and are equipped with the moral and social relationships needed to sustainably intervene. DIRCs also often engage in national advocacy on issues that are informed by local voices and needs. A key goal of their peace-building activities lies in stimulating collective responsiveness to the humanitarian needs of those in one's own community. DIRCs thus build and work within inter-religious efforts towards finding sustainable solutions to the effects of violence and disaster that remain in the post-war.

What is evident from the work of NPC is the reservoir of untapped goodwill that exists between the religious communities at the grassroots level. When religious leaders are brought together in structured initiatives they begin to better understand each other and to work together. In the northern capital of Jaffna, the Buddhist monk who is a member of the Jaffna DIRC has helped his colleagues from other religions to network with government authorities, including the army that effectively runs the north even after the war. The Jaffna DIRC has also gone as a group to make representations before the governor of the Northern Province and make appeals on behalf of people affected by problems that they cannot solve on their own. Another very successful activity has been exchange visits, whereby members of the interreligious committees go on cross-country visits to gain awareness of the issues that exist in other parts of the country.

In some ways, such work may be more effective in changing attitudes and at promoting peace than similar work among those at the public level. Unlike the leadership, the people have no concrete roles or agendas that prevent them from committing to a wholehearted stand for peace. Peace through the grassroots is also comparatively more stable, since it builds up a movement rather than trying to persuade multiple levels of the political, social, and religious hierarchies from the leadership and down. Most importantly, working at the grassroots bypasses the need to work through the very political structure that opposes peace; at the same time, it promotes a change in the hearts of the people, who together have the power to elect new leadership and change the state of the nation.

Grassroots' religious peace-building becomes further effective when there exists a large, strong religious network which is willing to support peace regardless of its current unpopularity. To appreciate the potential of self-motivated, faith-based actors at the grass roots, it is necessary to understand the existing religious infrastructure at this level. At present there are more than 30,000 Buddhist monks in the country serving approximately 75 percent of the population. Almost every village on the island has a Buddhist temple (excepting the North, though the growing Sinhala population in the East has also seen a corresponding rise in Buddhism). Thus, the reach of the Buddhist establishment is second only to the scope of the government. In light of this fact, Buddhist temples are largely untapped resources for peace-oriented advocacy at grassroots levels.

In regions where extensive and effective central government control is circumscribed, religion is also among the few institutions with some degree of popular credibility, trust and moral authority at the community level. When these assets are coupled with the personal direction that religious leaders offer their constituencies, these leaders become powerful advocates for peace, guiding the people in a personal and spiritual shift towards peaceful values. At a time when the people themselves are so ethnically and ideologically divided, the religious leaders have an especially important role to play in reconciliation. Their moral authority, along with the local power and resources they have access to means that any activism they engage in on behalf of the despondent minorities is also great.

Fortunately, Sri Lanka has the beginnings of a strong local religious movement for peace. President of the Sarvodaya Movement, Dr. A. T. Ariyaratne has experienced this in the numerous villages his organization has worked in. "Even without encouragement from the top leaders," he explained, "village level monks are self-motivated to participate in peace-building initiatives and to follow up their efforts."[26]

CRITIQUE AND ANALYSIS

Through both national institutions and grassroots programs therefore, religious-based peace work is on the rise. As these are, for the large part, fairly young initiatives there are yet many limitations and difficulties to be overcome.

The primary deterrent to success and productivity in the institutional interreligious movements are their own internal differences. Unfortunately, the religious leaders involved in these institutional assemblies cannot fully escape the historical politicization of religion and ethnicity, which prevents the formation of a truly cohesive movement. Their own segregated religious training prevents many from fully escaping the politicized ideas of "us" and "them" that are deeply embedded in Sri Lankan society. This makes it difficult for many religious leaders to truly empathize with the concerns of all ethno-religious groups and form a meaningful bond. In such a context, the composition of the interreligious groups also presents a problem. Within interreligious gatherings, Christians, Hindus and Muslims are a small minority, reflecting Sri Lanka's majoritarian political and social structure. Formal leadership in two of the three foremost interreligious peace groups (CoR and SLCRP)

26. Interview with A. T. Ariyaratne, October 21, 2008.

is also appropriated for Buddhist monks, who through both size and influence dominate the interreligious proceedings. However, their lack of enthusiasm to take on such a symbolically controversial and time-consuming role means that these organizations tend to lie dormant unless prodded by external actors.

Forming a movement that is both united in purpose and strengthened by resilient interreligious relationships is thus a challenging task. Increasing the complexity of current efforts are members' high profiles. As prominent leaders of the country's various religious groups, their values or actions are exposed to both internal and external critique. Some are subject to political patronage, meaning that they must be careful when sanctioning an ideal that is both politically vilified and generally perceived to be unrealistic (at present, there is a widespread lack of faith in a negotiated political solution due to the recent military success, and the unsuccessful track-record of negotiations in the past). When coupled with the individual prejudices that members may hold, these political pressures further prohibits internal unity and restricts interreligious peace-building.

Although the main objective of institutional religious peace organizations is to be a voice for peace, the various political standpoints of their members thus make it difficult for them to band together to confront the nationalistic leadership. According to the Bishop of Mannar, Rayappu Joseph, a prominent religious worker in the North, the peace-building capability of religious leaders is obstructed by their need for "political survival."[27] Since the current political context is often dangerous and uncertain, religious leaders must navigate a fine line between pleasing those in power and their own pro-peace ideals. This was very apparent during interreligious peace conferences, when, for example, Buddhist monks faced the challenge of defending the government's military solution to "terrorism" while calling for peace at the same time. In essence, the very influence and visibility that makes them prime national peacemakers is also the source of a major impediment to their peace work. As Dr. Ariyaratne reflects on this dual sword: "having national-level influence, while garnering great power also inculcates fear, prohibits unity and hinders the freedom to do what is right."[28] The powerful religious leaders who form the institutional interreligious peace movement must

27. Interview with R. Joseph, November 23, 2008.
28. Interview with A. T. Ariyaratne, October 21, 2008.

thus feel comfortable stepping past political boundaries, or must partner with lesser religious leaders who have the freedom to do so, if they are to progress in their quest for a peaceful Sri Lanka.

The prominent position and varying political beliefs of these religious leaders not only hinders internal accord, but also makes it difficult for them to fully commit to the time and mutual effort it takes to establish a religious movement. At present, there is little internal impetus among the three institutional peace organisations. It is common for outside actors to organize meetings and identify issues for religious leaders to engage with and undertake. Interactions take place on an ad hoc basis, and have not developed into sustained, meaningful relationships between religious groups. Furthermore, some top religious leaders are reluctant to get involved in their organization's activities unless they are persistently courted by community leaders. This lack of initiative and commitment among many of the top religious leaders significantly restricts the impact such a group could have. Not only does it prevent the group from developing into an independent body, but it presents a model of apathy that is in conflict with the active social conscience they are trying to inspire.

This lack of motivation also inhibits religious leaders from committing to significant action. Most activities organized by these interreligious organizations revolve most often around meetings and speeches and occasional statements to address pressing national issues. Workshops, conferences, and programs which promote sustainable peace and interreligious solidarity, however, are of no avail unless their ideas and plans are put into practice. As Douglas Johnston argues:

> [A]s popular as inter-religious dialogue has become as a proscribed remedy for reconciling strained relations . . . its perceived worth is probable overrated if it only amounts to ad hoc meetings and a sterile exchange of views about belief systems. If, however, it includes a mandate for action and a commitment to meet on an ongoing basis, then the relationships that result will likely lead to increased trust, at which point all things become possible.[29]

While institutional interreligious peace organisations have taken the initiative to engage in some level of action, they too have not been able to expand their activities into an extensive interreligious movement at the grassroots level. This could be because all three of these organizations

29. Johnston, "The Religious Dimensions of Peace-building," 8.

are relatively young; their emphasis therefore is on strengthening the movement and building it up. SLCRP has been establishing a network at the district level in order to connect top leaders with their grassroots counterparts. However, since these initiatives invariably operate through NGO-type funding, any action undertaken tends to become project focused and does not always prepare effectively for the long term.

Another impediment to the work of interreligious peace organizations is that there is no firm strategy to gradually build up a sustainable peace movement. Their plans and actions are undertaken erratically, to address a hot issue of the moment, or to vaguely strategize an unrelated series of events that add little to the development of the movement as a whole. Their efforts are further constrained by the fact that there is no solidarity between movements, even though all share a common goal of advancing peace and ethnic reconciliation. CoR, SLCRP, and IRPF all operate on their own (though members often participate in more than one organization). Field visits, writing statements, humanitarian work, and other tasks are all implemented independent of each other, with little dialogue or cooperation. Results are not shared, and thus organizations cannot learn from each other's accomplishments or mistakes. Furthermore, there is very little communication between top level religious movements and their spiritual counterparts at the grassroots. This fragments their work and impedes their success. This barrier between parallel interreligious groups is highly unfortunate, since it inhibits progress and defuses the immense power that a larger, multilevel interreligious coalition could have.

The lack of cohesion both within and across interreligious peace groups, their relative internal apathy and their inconsistent grassroots expansion means that these interreligious peace groups have not yet been able to develop a resilient peace movement that reaches all levels of society. The most formidable obstacle to their progress however, is the very same factor that prevents a successful negotiation of peace in Sri Lanka itself: these interreligious groups cannot attain a unified idea of "peace." While it is often claimed that all participating religious leaders want peace, this shared desire is often frustrated by their different, sometimes mutually exclusive understandings of peace as a process, a goal and an outcome. Many among the Buddhist leadership, for example, hold contradictory positions on the Sri Lankan conflict. The first is an avowed preference for nonviolence. The other is a commitment to a centralized government and unitary state (a standpoint that also openly conflicts with the motivations of ethnic minorities and thus negates the monks' potential for being nonpartisan intermediaries). Unfortunately, these political beliefs currently hold more influence over the Buddhist clergy. Their view of peace does not correspond with the ideals of power-sharing that other religious leaders hold, while their past political affiliation with the war undermines the trust necessary for being intermediaries for peace.

It is this failure to find a common ground that is harming the institutional interreligious peace-building effort the most. Members know that there are a number of differences between them, but they fear that addressing these differences will lead to conflict and damage the nascent movement. Since they have not been able to engage with each other and formulate a mutually inclusive ideal, they cannot take any decisive action or plan for the future. This failure to agree upon a mutual view of "peace" is also problematic since it reflects the incompatible attitudes within society—which are also the root of the civil war. If these organizations are to provide leadership in bringing peace to Sri Lanka, they *must* be able to reflect the solution within their own ranks to show that it is both possible and preferable. Otherwise, the unaddressed conflicts and growing division within them will become the very antithesis of the ideal they are seeking to project.

IMPLICATIONS FOR THEORY AND POLICY

Debates over the conflict in Sri Lanka have mainly focused on ethnic, economic and political grievances, as well as the manifestations and processes of armed challenges to the status quo. Much less attention has been paid to the question of how religious identity and resources may be linked to the development of conflict and how these factors may be mobilised in support of a sustainable peace settlement. In an effort to move the debate forward, we have argued that many theorists fail to identify how different axes of identity: such as religion are connected to the outbreak of "ethnic" conflicts. While a more detailed examination of these issues is needed, this chapter demonstrates that the prevailing discourse, which privileges ethnicity, is inadequate in the Sri Lankan case. Without such an understanding, lasting resolution of the Sri Lankan conflict remains difficult to envision.

The sustained efforts of religious leaders in post-conflict peace-building are crucial to the successful resolution of conflict. Interreligious peace initiatives offer a way to break down social boundaries and reconcile alienated communities. One important way they do this is through the utilisation of the pro-peace principles, shared by all religions, to promote solidarity and mutual understanding within society. This, in turn, has important implications for policy, which has long failed to overcome intergroup hostility and forge such cross-ethnic connections. Similarly, understanding how religious organizations can work to alleviate poverty and promote peace through development may also transform current policy approaches. Understanding and responding to conflict require a multifaceted, multilayered, and multi-actor methodology, in which religious leaders and initiatives form a crucial component. Four broad recommendations can be offered for strengthening interreligious peace organisations and incorporating them into development and peace-building policies.

First, an interreligious peace movement will need to come to an understanding of "peace" that all religious groups agree upon. It is vital that an honest discussion takes place between religious leaders who take part in this movement. The true implications of peace-building must be explored, while any threatening aspects of political change (such as the fear that the privileges accorded to Buddhism may diminish if there is any political power-sharing) must be addressed. If the religious leaders succeed in agreeing upon what is necessary for peace, it would enable them to commit to a clearly defined political goal. A shared objective is a necessary precondition for effective policy formulation. In addition, it would imply that they have undergone an attitudinal and behavioral change that is more conducive to their successful participation in peace-building.

Second, it is critical to invest in open, intimate discussion which includes informal and formal meetings, and conferences that take place at the national level. Such activities forge human relationships across religious lines, and may significantly contribute to the organizational strength of the movement. Increased internal unity would also translate into increased productivity as members use these relationships to address conflicts in their shared communities and work to plan and build peace together. However, at present donors of these organizations insist upon large-scale events that receive high publicity but which have very little impact. These events, which are organized by outside parties, often see little interaction between religious groups, even when they are all convened in the same group (dietary restrictions mean that some participants cannot even eat together). These events thus bear the semblance of unity, but in reality, they become a reflection of the division in society as a whole. To play an effective policy formulation role, these religious organizations thus require a better sense of their own institutional needs, capabilities, and limitations—far more than they do now.

Third, the movement must better integrate the work of its symbolically important members with grassroots-level religious leaders to fulfill the practical functions necessary for a peace movement. The current membership, though committed to the interreligious peace movement, cannot always spare the time and effort that building a new, nationwide movement requires. Religious leaders who occupy lower rungs of the religious hierarchy will prove crucial to these organizations, and the movement as a whole. Not only are they able to mobilize many of the same resources as their leadership, but they are also more available to take part in the intensive peace-building activities that the future will require. Furthermore, as the segment of the religious leadership that works most closely with the people, they will have the personal and influential relationships necessary to encourage peaceful values at the grassroots—an area in which the current peace movement has not yet had a broad impact. Ultimately, successful policy implementation will depend upon the infrastructure available at national, subnational *and* grassroots levels. Thus, without first strengthening this infrastructure interreligious initiatives have little hope of extending the scope of any movement for peace.

Finally, it is critical to expand the organizational and financial capacity of interreligious bodies to undertake development projects in partnership with local communities. By doing so, interreligious and religious organizations may slowly transform the status quo in which many decisions affecting the poor and marginalized ignore beneficiary input. Most importantly, such participatory processes can facilitate consensus-building and social interaction among different groups which are not only crucial for economic development but also, more broadly, reconciliation and sustainable peace. One of the great virtues of interreligious initiatives, which should be incorporated into broader peace and development policies, is their ability to tap into a common language for different groups, enabling them to communicate more easily with one another.

CONCLUSION

Although some time has passed since the military defeat of the LTTE, no substantial efforts have been made to conciliate the minority groups either politically or ideologically. In light of the continued violence and ethnic tension in "post-war" Sri Lanka, the existence of these interreligious movements has proved most fortunate. As all nascent movements, they have encountered some obstacles which have initially impeded their progress. However, with religious values being one of the few commonalities between the divided ethnic groups, such movements will be essential in encouraging dialogue and fostering peace. The next stage of this movement, its organizational development, coincides with a critical period in the country's history. The victory of government troops may signify the end of military activity, but the political trend of ignoring minority grievances may renew ethnic tensions in the medium to long term. The interreligious peace movement will thus be more necessary than ever. If the organizations driving this movement could encourage an internal unity based on mutual values and work together towards building peace at all levels of society, they could become an influential force in the field of post-conflict reconciliation. The interreligious peace movement could thus help heal this war-weary society, gradually transforming Sri Lanka into a land where people transcend social divides and live in peace and harmony.

BIBLIOGRAPHY

Literature

Bartholomeusz, Tessa. *In Defense of Dharma: Just War Ideology in Buddhist Sri Lanka.* New York: Routledge, 2002.

———. "In Defense of Dharma: Just War Ideology in Buddhist Sri Lanka." *Journal of Buddhist Ethics* 6 (1999) 1–16.

Bilodeau, Alex. *The Inter-Religious Peace Foundation: Christians, Muslims, Buddhists and Hindus—Addressing the Conflict in Sri Lanka.* Cambridge, MA: Reflecting on Peace Practice Project, 2000.

Bouta, Tsjeard S., Asye Kadayifci-Orellana, and Mohammed Abu-Nimer. *Faith-Based Peace-Building: Mapping and Analysis of Christian, Muslim and Multi-Faith Actors.* Washington DC: Clingendael Institute, 2005.

Bush, Kenneth D. *The Intra-Group Dimensions of Ethnic Conflict in Sri Lanka: Learning to Read Between the Lines*. New York: Palgrave Macmillan, 2003.

De Silva, K. M. *A History of Sri Lanka*. Colombo: Sri Lanka: Vijitha Yapa, 2003.

———. *Reaping the Whirlwind: Ethnic Conflict, Ethnic Politics in Sri Lanka*. New Delhi: Penguin, 1998.

———. "Regionalism and Decentralisation of Power." In *Sri Lanka: Problems of Governance*, edited by K. M. De Silva, 103–8. New Delhi: Centre for Policy Research, 1993.

DeVotta, Neil. *Blowback: Linguistic Nationalism, Institutional Decay, and Ethnic Conflict in Sri Lanka*. Stanford: Stanford University Press, 2004.

———. "Control Democracy, Institutional Decay, and the Quest for Eelam: Explaining Ethnic Conflict in Sri Lanka." *Pacific Affairs* 73/1 (2000) 55–76.

———. "From Ethnic Outbidding to Ethnic Conflict: The Institutional Bases for Sri Lanka's Separatist War." *Nations and Nationalism* 11/1 (2005) 150–59.

Flanigan, Shawn Teresa. "Faith and Fear in Development: The Role of Religion in Sri Lanka's NGO Sector." Paper Presented at the ISA's 49th Annual Convention: Bridging Multiple Divides, San Francisco, 2008. Online: http://www.allacademic.com/meta/p254098_index.html.

Imtiyaz, A. R. M., and Ben Stavis. "Ethno-Political Conflict in Sri Lanka." *Journal of Third World Studies* 25/2 (2008) 135–52.

Johnston, Douglas. "The Religious Dimensions of Peacebuilding." In *People Building Peace II: Successful Stories of Civil Society*, edited by Paul Van Tongeren et al. London: Lynne Rienner, 2005.

Manoharan, Nagaio. *Democratic Dilemma: Ethnic Violence and Human Rights in Sri Lanka*. New Delhi: Samskriti, 2008.

Peebles, Patrick. *The History of Sri Lanka*. London: Greenwood, 2006.

Peleg, Ilan. *Democratizing the Hegemonic State: Political Transformation in the Age of Identity*. Cambridge: Cambridge University Press, 2007.

Population by Ethnicity, Census Years. Colombo, Sri Lanka: Department of Census and Statistics, 2008.

Rajapaksa, Mahinda. "Address by HE President Mahinda Rajapaksa at the Ceremonial Opening of Parliament, Sri Jawardhanapura (19 May 2009)." Online: http://www.president.gov.lk/speech_New.asp?Id=74.

Rodrigo, K. "World Religious Leaders' Great Enthusiasm for Peace in Sri Lanka." Speech given at the Inaugural Conference of the Inter Religious Council of Sri Lanka. April 28, 2008.

Orjuela, Camilla. *Civil Society in Civil War: Peace Work and Identity Politics in Sri Lanka*. Gothenberg, Sweden: Department of Peace and Development Research, 2004.

Sabaratnam, Lakshmanan. *Ethnic Attachments in Sri Lanka: Social Change and Cultural Continuity*. New York: Palgrave, 2001.

Smock, David R. *Religious Contributions to Peacemaking: When Religion Brings Peace, Not War*. Washington D.C.: United States Institute of Peace, 2006.

Van Tongeren, Paul, Malin Brenk, Marte Hellema, and Juliette Verhoeven, eds. *People Building Peace II: Successful Stories of Civil Society*. London: Lynne Rienner, 2005.

Wellman, James K., Jr., and Kyoko Tokuno. "Is Religious Violence Inevitable?" *Journal for the Scientific Study of Religion* 43 (2004) 291–96.

7

"Peacemakers" from the "Bridge Church"

The Anglican Church as A Third Party
in Palestine 1920–1948

MARIA SMÅBERG

The policy of the Anglican communion to promote mutual understanding and goodwill, not only between various branches of
the Christian Church, but also between the religious leaders of
Islam and Judaism, has enabled the Bishopric to obtain a valuable
insight into the religious questions, and frequently the Bishop or
his advisers have been asked to give counsel in matters where a
mediator has been necessary.[1]

Bishop Graham-Brown to Secretary of State for Colonies
and Dominions MacDonald, November 29, 1938

During the British Mandate period in Palestine, Jewish, Muslim, and
Christian religious leaders met and prayed together for peace at
the Anglican Cathedral in Jerusalem. At this time Jerusalem bore all the
imprints of ethnic and religious separation and division. The Anglican
Church viewed itself as a "Bridge Church" as well as "mediator" and
"peacemaker" who wanted to promote what we today would call conflict
transformation and peace-building in Palestine. However, this role was
ambiguous. The Anglican Church had no official status as a "third party"
chosen by the conflicting parties. Rather, it was intertwined with the
Mandate regime, making it impossible to be neutral. Nonetheless, they

1. *The Jerusalem and East Mission (J&EM) Papers* LXI/4: Letter from Graham-
Brown to MacDonald, November 29, 1938.

took upon themselves a symbolic role of mediation in civil society. This unofficial role as a third party is what I will explore and discuss.

We will focus on an early example of faith-based diplomacy.[2] The religious sector may well be the most rapidly expanding one, in the field of international conflict analysis today.[3] Using a modern theoretical framework, which connects religion and international politics, opens up for interesting interpretations of historical material. This study is analyzing, for instance, the statements and actions taken by the Anglican bishops in Jerusalem, the official representatives of the Anglican Church in Palestine. During the British Mandate period, three persons served as Anglican bishops in Jerusalem: Rennie MacInnes (1914–1931), George Francis Graham-Brown (1932–1942), and Weston Henry Stewart (1943–1957). They were all British.[4] Thus, the discourses and activities on a general and elite level in order to reach the overall ideology of the Anglican Church are here in focus, revealing a discourse that implies Anglican aims and structures of thinking.[5]

When looking into the discourses and activities, both formal and informal peace efforts are highlighted: interfaith rituals and relations, advocacy and mediation. Two lines of interpretation are here emphasized: one focusing on the Anglican discourses and activities as evident part of British spiritual and political imperialism, the other taking seriously the efforts of the Anglicans trying to be an informal "third party" who promoted interreligious dialogue and faith-based diplomacy in civil society.

---

2. Faith-based diplomacy assumes that religious faith can be a catalyst for peacemaking, instead of a basis for conflict. See Johnston, *Faith-Based*.

3. Sampson notes for example: "What for decades was the untold, unnoticed story behind the new—the undocumented history of religiously motivated peacemaking and reconciliation efforts—has now begun to grab the attention of scholars, journalists, diplomats, various governmental and nongovernmental agencies, and funding organizations as these efforts have become more numerous, more visible, and more needed" (Sampson, "Religion," 273).

4. The first Anglican Arab to become appointed Anglican Bishop was Najib Qub'ayn in 1958. In 1976 Fi'iq Haddad was ordained the first Anglican Arab Archbishop in Jerusalem and the Middle East. See Tsimhoni, *Christian Communities*, 142–45.

5. Said, *Orientalism*, 23–24, 122. I assume that the Anglicans' statements about issues connected to peace and conflict are expressions of various forms of thinking which can be ranged within a broader pattern of religious and imperialist assumptions and established "truths" which, in turn, are expressions of power.

IN THE MIDST OF CONFLICT

The Anglican Church's presence in the Holy Land started in 1841 when the Anglo-Prussian Episcopal See was established in Jerusalem. During the nineteenth century, Western tourists, pilgrims, missionaries, scholars, and diplomats arrived there due to Christian revivalism, Great Power politics as well as improved communications. The Anglican missionary organizations worked in the fields of education, health care, and charity with the object to win Jewish, Muslim, and Eastern Christian souls as well as to contribute to the welfare of the region. The Anglicans changed the missionary course, which had not succeeded at all, already at the end of the nineteenth century. Instead of trying to convert people with other religious background, they now wished to create "friendly relations" with them. Multicultural schools in particular were a part of this new project with the function of being a test-place for interreligious coexistence.[6]

At the peace conferences after World War I with the ensuing Mandate system, the newly founded League of Nations took the decision to leave the administration of Palestine to United Kingdom. The region, which had for a long time been a part of the Ottoman Empire, now became a British Mandate. However, the takeover was not meant to be of enduring character. All Mandate powers were obliged to lead the mandate territories towards self-government, and as for Palestine it was considered that this should be fulfilled in a near future. However, the mandate in Palestine faced uncertainties and contradictions. Already during World War I the British had given promises both to Arabs and Jews about a future autonomy or a national home. But what did those promises mean? It soon became evident that the contradictions they created could not be resolved. There were at the same time many splits within the Palestinian society: different fractions, classes, families, and religious groups, as well as contrasting urban and rural areas. The greatest antagonism, however, was that between Zionist and Palestinian-Arab nationalist groups. The situation deteriorated and violence escalated, most poignantly in the 1930s and onwards. Zionists, whose ideals were fixed on Palestine, wanted massive Jewish immigration and the eventual

---

6. Wasserstein, *Divided Jerusalem*; Okkenhaug, *The Quality of Heroic Living*; and Shepherd, *The Zealous*.

creation of a Jewish state. Palestinian Arabs on the other hand wanted no further Jewish immigration and definitely no Jewish state.[7]

The idea behind the Mandate system was to find a solution through negotiations. Also the Anglican Church promoted an idea of a common Palestinian identity and a community transgressing borders. In Palestine, however, the situation grew even worse. Neither side would cooperate with the British in their efforts to create a united Palestine. The British lost control of the situation and, in 1947, returned the mandate to the successor of the League of Nations, the United Nations.[8]

Drawing on these historical facts, it is obvious that the British representatives of the Anglican Church faced severe challenges in Palestine. The British official task was to try to preserve peace in Palestine, giving in neither to Jewish nor Arab pressure. The Anglicans had to work under extremely difficult circumstances, being just as vulnerable as everyone else to riots in the streets. At the same time they brought with them the ideas of British justice and political superiority, and they were Christians at heart. Thus, it is a delicate task to try to interpret an important part of the British endeavor in Jerusalem—the discourses and activities of the Anglican Church—in the midst of dramatic intercommunal clashes.

RELIGIOUS ACTORS FOR PEACE IN CIVIL SOCIETY

Faith-based diplomacy is based on the idea that religious leaders and their network enjoy certain comparative advantages in contrast to official diplomats.[9] These actions can be connected to diplomacy on a track II (informal) and track III (secret) level. On these levels a set of activities and frameworks are designed to informally support formal negotiation and peace process.[10] Not only official representatives are included in

7. See e.g., Wasserstein, *The British* and Morris, *Righteous*.

8. Marshall, "The History," 82.

9. Johnston, *Faith-Based* and Scheffler, "Interfaith Dialogue," 3–4. According to Scheffler, the scholarly interest in "faith-based diplomacy" arose in 1980s and 1990s and was inspired by the role of religious leaders in effecting the smooth regime change in Eastern Europe and the Philippines; by the success of groups like the Community San'Egidio in negotiating peace agreements, and the role of religious leaders in establishing for instance the Truth and Reconciliation Commission in South Africa.

10. Ramsbotham, Woodhouse, and Miall, *Contemporary*, 21–30, 180–88. See also Aggestam, *Reframing*, on Israeli-Palestinian negotiations between 1988 and 1998 and the use of different tracks in the negotiation strategies. She emphasises the track-two diplomacy which is described as "unofficial and informal negotiations outside gov-

such diplomatic negotiations, but also non-state actors such as NGO workers, religious leaders, and private citizens.

Religion, though, is often tainted with nationalism and therefore sometimes seen as part of the problem more than the solution in a conflict. In Palestine, religion was an important marker of identity and social belonging, a heritage stemming from the *millet*-system established during the Ottoman period. The British took over the *millet* system. It was, for instance, based on local autonomy for religious groups.[11] The status of the individual was derived from his/her membership of a protected religious community, *millet*, headed by a *millet-basi* (a patriarch or a chief rabbi) who, in addition to his spiritual leadership, was responsible to the state for the administration of his community. Hence, the basis of the law was personal rather than territorial and religious rather than national or ethnic.[12] Even the British Mandate based its policy of creating political alliances with the local elite and the religious institutions. Thus, religion also had political implications to a great extent. Moreover, often religion was used as a legitimizing force for conflict and violence.[13]

As a complementing image to this role of religion in the conflict, we can note that also attitudes tending towards interfaith dialogue and faith-based peace activism are to be found in the ideology of the Anglican Church in Mandatory Palestine. However, by investigating the interplay of the two opposites of colonial oppression and religious dialogue, the complex implications of such activism become evident.

The issue how popular engagement in political life and strengthening the civil society can contribute to conflict resolution has become more topical. Side by side with the rigid and stereotyped views of "the

ernment structures" (178–81). Concerning the track III level, the scholars Joseph Montville, Elise Boulding, Adam Curle and John Paul Lederach are often referred to.

11. Stillman, *The Jews*, 97 and Tsimhoni, "The Status," 166. The millet system was based on the tradition of Islam, tolerating non-Muslims who recognised the books of divine revelation, *ahl al-kitab* (the people of the Book). Jews and Christians were tolerated as *dhimmis* (protected people), which meant that these groups were granted protection for their lives and liberties and were allowed to practice their own religion. In return, the Muslims demanded submission under Muslim rulers, special taxes (the *jizya* and the *kharaj*, the poll tax and the land tax) and certain restrictions to mark their inferiority (such as wearing distinctive clothing and the prohibition of carrying arms and riding horses).

12. Tsimhoni, "The Status," 166.

13. See i.e., Mattar, *The Mufti*; Kolinsky, *Law*; Elpeleg, *The Grand*; Sela, "The 'Wailing Wall'"; Smith, *Palestine*; Lewis, *The Multiple*; and Cohen, *Saving*.

other" there exists as well often transgressing and inclusive images. Mary Kaldor calls such groups "civilians," who refrain from adopting the negative stereotypes of official discourses, i. e., who do not affirm an excluding policy. Therefore, according to Kaldor, in order to promote conflict resolution and reconciliation, a "cosmopolitan" culture must be advocated, fostering inclusiveness instead of plans for exclusion or separation. Such cosmopolitanism is found among the NGOs and grassroots in the civil society, Kaldor claims.[14]

Also the relationship between the church and civil society has been increasingly in focus, including interfaith efforts to peace-building.[15] As a state church, the Anglican Church was of course associated with the British state and empire. Its close connection to the British rulers is evident. The Anglican Church in Palestine saw itself as the "spiritual arm" of the Mandate regime and the "unifying force of the Empire."[16] However, it was also related to civil institutions through its work with education, health care, and social reforms. In this way it was a provider of services and even an agent of social justice, acting in the interests of disadvantaged groups. Different examples from the past show how Anglican missionaries criticized the empire and joined forces with the locals.[17] Recent research therefore argues that missionaries are not only to be viewed as imperial agents, but also as agents for social reforms.[18]

14. Kaldor, *New*, 138. See also Kaldor, *Global*. However, there are many problems and risks with such an approach. See for example Chandler, *Bosnia*, and Paris, *At War's*, who discuss the risk of a gap between the NGOs and the ordinary local man and woman, as the NGOs tend to become too internationally influenced, urban centered, and middle-class based. In civil society also exists spoiler groups opposing peace processes.

15. For a discussion about the relationship between the church and "civil society," see i.e., Fergusson, *Church*, and Tejirian, "Faith." For interreligious efforts and conflict resolution, see i.e., Smock, *Religious*, and *Interfaith*; Johnston, *Faith-Based*; Abu-Nimer, "Religion"; and Scheffler, "Interfaith." American political scientist Robert D. Putnam's *Bowling Alone* has promoted the idea that civil society, civic culture, and social capital are important for strengthening democracy and enabling conflict resolution. However, Putnam strongly rejects religion as a factor that can aid civic society; organized religion is, in fact, unfavorable to civil society, he argues. See Putnam, Leonardi, and Nanetti, *Making*.

16. Cragg, "The Anglican"; Okkenhaug, *The Quality of Heroic Living*; Shepherd, *Ploughing*; and Småberg, *Ambivalent*.

17. Stanley, *The Bible*; Washbrook, "Orients"; Porter, "Empires"; Etherington, "Missions"; Louis, "Introduction"; and Owen, "Critics."

18. Okkenhaug, *Gender*.

Also Anglican Bishopric in Jerusalem played a dual role during the mandate period. It served British and American residents and visitors, but also local Arab Christians and a few Hebrew Christians.[19] One example will be mentioned to highlight the dual situation. Within the Anglican Church there was a group of local Anglican Arabs with an Arab clergy. In the Palestine Native Church Council, local clergy united with laity to establish a self-governing, self-supporting system.[20] Thus, being Anglican did not necessarily mean being British. However, Bishop Abu El-Assal mentions in an article on the history of the Anglican Church in Palestine that Arab Anglicans were influenced by the British with respect to the design of the church building, the prayer books and services, as well as life style in general. Some Arab Anglicans even insisted on taking high tea at four o'clock Greenwich Mean Time.[21] The Anglican Arab group, in turn, influenced the Anglican establishment as well as the British officials. This was an effect of the social contacts that developed within the parish life between Palestinian Arabs, identifying with the Palestinian Arab national cause, and British officials.[22]

The government in Palestine insisted on equal treatment of the two communities, a policy that was also followed by the Anglican Bishop in Jerusalem, according to Okkenhaug.[23] Still, the Anglican Church's close contacts with Christian Arabs led to an Arab bias among the Anglicans as well as the British officials in general. The Anglican Bishop acted as a spokesperson for the Arab population. Okkenhaug argues that the Anglicans' interventions "behind the scenes" resulted in a general tendency to see the Anglican Church as "an alternative, morally sound British authority in contrast to the Mandate government" in the 1930s.[24]

19. Tsimhoni, *Christian*, 139–40.

20. Abu El-Assal, "The Birth," 131–32.

21. Ibid., 137.

22. Wasserstein, *The British*.

23. Okkenhaug, *The Quality of Heroic Living*, 119.

24. After a high ranking British official in Galilee had been murdered in 1936, Bishop Graham-Brown intervened to the High Commissioner on behalf of the Muslim parents of the main suspect. The Christian Arabs asked Bishop Graham-Brown to represent them at the Peel Commission hearings when the Arab Higher Committee had decided to boycott the hearings. Okkenhaug, *The Quality of Heroic Living*, 124–29, 131–34. See also Tsimhoni, *Christian*, 139–40; Lang Papers, 52/112; and The Jerusalem and East Mission Papers LXI/2. Bishop Graham-Brown also made appeals on behalf of a Jewish farm school, see The Jerusalem and East Mission Papers LXII/2.

Thus, we can already identify an Anglican ambiguity in regard to British imperialism and towards local Palestinian nationalism.

John Paul Lederach recognizes how peace-building efforts may become a complement for traditional mediation on an official government-to-government level. His famous pyramid design (1997) is helpful when evaluating peace-building on different levels in a society, from "top-down" and "bottom-up." He recognizes actors on elite, middle range, and grassroots levels. To provide a structure for reconciliation, Lederach recommends coordinating the peacemaking efforts of the actors on the different levels. Leaders at the middle range level then become central. Their position between the top and the grassroots levels makes them suitable to facilitate communication between both. Many scholars and practitioners argue that this level should get more attention and resources.[25]

At the middle range position, the Anglican Church had contacts with various local leaders on all three levels. In the following parts I will investigate the Anglican peace-building efforts further through a study limited to the bishops' relations. The church, however, conducted work on many levels involving i.e., health care, education, military and police forces. This made for various contacts with the local population, which is not explicit when only studying the bishops.[26]

Thus, in the understanding of the Anglican peace efforts, the Anglican representatives in Palestine can be seen as actors in the civil society. In doing so, we can connect to the process thinking of modern peace-building and conflict transformation theory, focusing on encounters and communication between actors on various levels in order to reduce the impact of stereotypes and to build up trust between people

25. Lederach, *Building Peace*, 37–55. The top-level concerns political and military leaders who generally negotiate cease-fires and peace accords. Their social position makes them influential bringing about reforms from top-down. Middle range leaders (e.g., leaders of academic, religious, business, professional, agricultural, and nongovernmental organizations) conduct and engage in problem solving workshops, train people in conflict resolution skills, and lead peace commissions. At the bottom of the pyramid we find the grassroots leaders. They are usually deeply involved in the conflict through work as community and refugee camp leaders, health officers, and members of indigenous nongovernmental organizations. The grassroots leaders concentrate on the bottom-up approach.

26. For a broader study of the Anglican Church in Palestine, see Småberg, *Ambivalent*.

of different groups.[27] However, there is no intention to test the theories through examples from the past. Rather they are heuristic tools in order to sharpen certain tendencies in the material that otherwise might not have been seen.

Let us now look deeper into the different means of peacemaking which the Anglican Church promoted and the beliefs and values behind these religious peace efforts. Interfaith rituals and relations as well as advocacy and mediation will be discussed. I will especially take notice of and differentiate between the formal and informal means used.

CEREMONIAL MEETINGS

Marc Gopin highlights communication and relationship-building in conflict resolution. He distinguishes between two kinds of personal engagement: (1) informal and (2) formal or ritualistic. Both are vital for the result of conflict resolution, he argues. Religious leaders have emphasized these two kinds of human engagement differently. To some, high-level relationship-building between religious leadership is focused, with emphasis on formal contacts and conversation. Others have promoted the slow growth of interpersonal relationships over time between key figures of opposing groups, as well as direct emotional appeals.[28]

Among the formal means used by the Anglicans, we find official prayers and services. Throughout the mandate period, the Anglicans invited other religious as well as secular representatives to prayers and services in the Anglican cathedral. For example in 1939, the Anglican Church in Jerusalem arranged a national prayer. Other religious leaders as well as leaders of the Mandate administration attended the worships to pray for the situation in Europe, for peace of the world and for the Christian church. Every year during World War II, the Anglicans continued to assemble representatives of all communities to pray with them on a National Prayer Day.

However, it is interesting to look deeper into what the Anglican Church made of such an occasion on which all groups were gathered. Since it was such a public prayer it also leans towards being a ritual, *alas* making the concept of prayer more complex. Rituals can be seen as

27. See Lederach, *Building Peace*; and Ramsbotham, Woodhouse, and Miall, *Contemporary*.

28. Gopin, *Holy*, 161.

nonverbal communication and performative actions.[29] On the National Prayer Day, Sunday May 26, 1940, the intercession was formed as follows. The service started with an Anglican hymn: "O God, our help in ages past . . ." In the introduction that followed, it was declared that the visitors were seen as brethren and that they had met in the sight of God to intercede:

> . . . for the World, for our own Nation and Empire, for our Allies, and for the cause in which we are united . . . and humbly submit to the protection and blessing of Almighty God the just cause to which with its Allies our Nation has pledged itself. It is God's will that we seek, and we have the assurance of His desire and His power to accomplish it.[30]

In times of world war, the Anglican prayers at a service for all communities, dealt with the British nation and empire, its allies and their just cause. It is possible to understand these nationalistic prayers as a wish to stand united in the times of war. However, the Anglican Church imposed on the visitors its own points of view, and it was done in an emotional way in the form of prayers. In this sense, a construction of hegemonic power was expressed in this prayer, and in the service.

The ceremony continued with the Lord's Prayer, the most characteristic Christian prayer of all. Then Psalm 46 was read, a text focusing the almighty God as strength and a helper. The Psalms are a part of the Bible which the Christians share with the Jews. The Anglicans obviously chose such a text instead of one from the New Testament. After a "recessional" (song), the National Anthem was sung and the service was concluded with the blessing.[31] Francis Younghusband, the leader of the

29. For a discussion on the interpretation of rituals, see Bell, *Ritual*. Professor Ronald L. Grimes reports on ritual studies in the *Encyclopedia of Religion* (1987) that recent research, instead of viewing rituals as normative expressions of a doctrine, study how rituals function and influence the actors, what the ritual transmits, and how the participants in a ritual interact, and how they experience and interpret it. The message of the ritual is part of the interaction and can be interpreted as a strategy of power and social control. The ritual may also be connected to non-cognitive performance and ethics. Among other things, rituals can also function as therapy. See Hjärpe, "Religionshistorikern," 303–7.

30. The Jerusalem and East Mission Papers LXVII/2: "Correspondence and memoranda *re* services of intercession, days of prayers for peace, etc. 1939–43." A form of intercession to be used on a day of national prayer Sunday, May 26, 1940.

31. Ibid. According to the archive material similar prayers were held on September 8, 1940, March 23, 1941, September 7, 1941, March 29, 1942, and September 3, 1943.

World Congress of Faiths at that time, saw in national prayers a way for the nations of the world "to be united in a firmer fellowship for the good of all mankind."[32] However, in spite of all good intentions to gather people from all communities to pray for peace, the form of this service and the structure of the prayers are rather excluding. True, the prayers were translated into Arabic and a text from the Old Testament was chosen, but its form was predominantly British and Christian.

Scholars of social closure theory, such as Raymond Murphy, study the strategies used by certain groups in a society to distinguish themselves from other groups in order to monopolize certain benefits or resources. Such strategies include rituals, according to Murphy.[33] However, in such cases there is a consciousness of, and a clear wish to, include some and exclude others. In our case there is no such conscious or outspoken aim of exclusion. On the contrary, the aim is integration. Yet the effect of the rituals is exclusionary.

The reactions to these national days of prayers were however positive. Supportive letters were sent to the Anglican Bishop by leaders of other churches. The Latin Patriarch wrote about "the important function" of prayer for peace.[34] The Greek Orthodox Patriarchate arranged similar prayers at their centers all over Palestine.[35] It is indeed interesting to notice the existence of a social network between the religious leaders, giving each other support in matters concerning prayers for peace. It might, in fact, also have been a strategy behind this support from the local groups, wishing to be on good terms with the representatives of the ruling regime.

Rituals can be used as means to construct power and difference, but also to articulate compromises and healing of conflicts, according to i.e., Gluckman and Geertz.[36] With such perspective rituals become a valuable part of peace-building.

32. Braybrooke, A Sider, 51–52.

33. Murphy, Social.

34. The Jerusalem and East Mission Papers LXVII/2: "Correspondence and memoranda re services of intercession, days of prayers for peace, etc. 1939–43." Letter from the Latin Patriarch to Graham-Brown, March 17, 1941.

35. Ibid. Note from George Said, September 1, 1941. A similar note was sent March 25, 1943.

36. See for example Gluckman, "Les rites de passage," 20–24; Geertz, Negara, 112; and Geertz, The Interpretation, 110–11.

The Anglicans gathered a great number of people from other communities at a service on December 9, 1920, celebrating the anniversary of the liberation of Jerusalem by Lord Allenby in 1917. The service was actually held as the government's official service of thanksgiving. Later, Bishop MacInnes recounts that during the course of the sermon he spoke about the differences between the groups present, but also about the remarkable fact that they had all gathered in a church. Prayers were said in Arabic and Hebrew and passages of the Bible were read in Hebrew, Greek and English by representatives of various religious communities as well as the British troops, and by the British governor.[37]

Looking at this event from today's perspective, it is not obvious that all groups experienced the British conquest of Jerusalem in 1917 as "liberation" worth commemorating. This remark notwithstanding, it is an example of ideas of integration and inclusiveness being transmitted by the bishops. All religious groups are invited, various languages are used and representatives from various directions are engaged in the ceremony. However, the diversity and differences are openly confronted in the bishop's sermon, thus following for example Max Gluckman's ideas on the function of praising unity in rituals in order to nourish social relations.[38] The differences are not used as a marker to exclude others and point out who does not belong. A friendly understanding, striving towards a universal human community, is the overruling aim expressed by the bishop. A belief that there can be diversity without enmity is assumed.

On the theme "Peace Making in Palestine" in a broadcast on June 6, 1937, Bishop Graham-Brown mentions other kinds of meetings, such as the more or less ritualized receptions in his house:

> So you can see that the Bishop's drawing room becomes the meeting place of the religions in their divisions and subdivisions, which hold the Holy Land sacred. For us all to meet together is a real bit of peace-making![39]

There was obviously an aim to create direct contact between religious leaders and build up relations in various ways.

---

37. *Bible Lands* VI, 1923, 297: "Liberation Day in Jerusalem."
38. Gluckman, "Les rites de passage," 20–24.
39. *Bible Lands* IX, 1937, 876–880: "Peace Making in Palestine."

When religious leaders in Jerusalem met in the Anglican surroundings, they did it on Anglican terms and within a framework of an assumed Christian superiority. However, it is most likely that the Anglicans had to adjust to other churches' traditions and norms when paying visits to other churches. In the rituals we also find ambivalence. The Anglican rituals conveyed power, while simultaneously articulating a quest for conflict transformation and healing, when aiming at communication, friendship, participation of all and relation building among religious leaders. The Anglican Church's views of rituals came close to those of a third party trying to support other religious leaders. Our task is now to investigate in what way the Anglicans also took a step further, turning interfaith dialogue into political action.

ADVOCATE FOR MINORITY GROUPS

According to Gopin, "third parties must come to believe that the elite are both more powerful and less powerful than they think they are." In Gopin's eyes the elites are less powerful than they know, in the sense that they find it difficult to believe just how constrained they are by the will of the majority. They must submit to the masses of their people and acknowledge their rage, instead of manipulating them and try to outmaneuver their basic sensibilities. On the other hand, leaders have far greater capacity than they think to heal the masses and to truly lead a civilization, Gopin argues. "It is the third party's obligation to help leaders see their true potential and also realistically assess what it will take for the majority of their people to come to a political space of peace and justice."[40] Thus, following Gopin, there could be much potential in religious leaders' actions for reconciliation and peace, a potential that may also spread a spirit of peace and justice to the political sphere.[41]

The Anglican Church's role as a third party is particularly evident in the case of the Palestine Royal Commissions interviews with various groups in Palestine in 1937.[42] In a letter to Archbishop Lang on January

40. Gopin, *Holy*, 225–26.

41. Ibid.

42. The commission was set up under Lord Peel in order to determine the causes of the conflict and find a way of dealing with the grievances of both Arabs and Jews. The Arabs, however, boycotted the commission until just before its departure. In 1937 the commission published its recommendations, stating that coexistence was impossible and that partition was the only solution.

15, 1937, Bishop Graham-Brown reports from his "evidence" to the commission. Since none of the Christian religious heads were prepared to participate, the Anglican Bishop saw himself as their spokesperson.[43] In his evidence Graham-Brown emphasized the spiritual dimensions from a Christian universalist point of view and pleaded for a common moral denominator based on the Golden Rule:

> . . . I preached two sermons, one emphasizing the fact that the people in Palestine were stewards for the three monotheistic religions and that Our Lord taught us by example true relationship to nationalism . . . that in Jesus Christ "there is neither Jew nor Greek." In the second sermon I plead for the establishment of a common moral denominator for the regulation of life in this country . . . and this I urged should be love of God and love of one's neighbor as oneself.[44]

With this statement, the bishop takes a stand for a moral and spiritual road forward in the framework of peacemaking. The bishop deplores the secularization of ideals on the part of all, Jews, Arabs, British, and argues that the present dominance of material considerations over spiritual principles was one of the underlying causes, if not the main cause, of the disturbances. Moreover, he expresses his personal views on many political matters including the conceivable solutions to the problems of Palestine. Among many things, he urges that a religious advisory council to the government be set up.[45] When discussing political matters he brings with him a moral and religious perspective which he also seems locked into.

As a spokesperson, Graham-Brown points at the grievances of the Christians. He also criticizes the government, holding that "the government unwittingly serves Mammon and has forgotten to serve God; spiritual and cultural interests have been sacrificed to economic

43. In a letter to Archbishop Lang on January 21, 1937, Graham-Brown mentions the enquires from Arabs and Jews in connection with the Royal Commission hearings: "I have been in frequent touch both with Arabs and Jews, but my closest relations have been with the former. Indeed, special envoys were sent to me on two occasions, asking me to help." Lang Papers, 52/137: Letter from Graham-Brown to Lang, January 21, 1937. Also in The Jerusalem and East Mission Papers LXI/2.

44. Lang Papers 52/112: Letter from Graham-Brown to Lang, January 15, 1937. Also in The Jerusalem and East Mission Papers LXI/2.

45. Lang Papers 52/112: Letter from Graham-Brown to Lang, January 15, 1937. Also in The Jerusalem and East Mission Papers LXI/2.

considerations." The bishop also criticizes his own government for not doing enough, and for committing injustices: "the Government has failed to bring communities together and to stimulate common understanding and interest; their policy has encouraged national and racial antagonism."[46] Contrary to the British partition plans, the bishop gives voice to a solution based on coexistence between Jews and Arabs. In this case, the bishop sees his role of a third party as that of being an advocate for minorities, the Christian Arabs as well as the Hebrew Christians, and giving legitimacy to the religious, moral and cultural needs of a country.[47]

FRIEND AND FACILITATOR

Bishop Graham-Brown connected his role as a spokesperson with the task of a mediator. It can be argued that the bishop even saw an opportunity to informally develop trust between the parties, to govern the situation and the context where the meetings took place, and facilitate the communication between the parties.[48] The informal receptions at the Bishop's home can be interpreted in this context. The receptions were given for the heads of all the religious communities: Christian, Muslim, and Jewish, to meet unofficially with the members of the Royal Commission. Bishop Graham-Brown writes to Archbishop Lang on January 21, 1937:

> In this country I had to explain that I was inviting some of my friends to meet other of my friends. All the religious heads responded very warmly, the only one who refused was the Mufti, because the boycott of the Commission had not yet been lifted. Actually, the Mufti came and had tea with us on Christmas Day: I would not say "instead," but to show his friendship.[49]

Here the word "friendship" is used, a word closely connected to informal relations. In a work on nonviolence, Curle points to one aspect of the role of a mediator: to be a friend. He highlights the fact that a mediator

---

46. Lang Papers 52/112: Letter from Graham-Brown to Lang, January 15, 1937. Also in The Jerusalem and East Mission Papers LXI/2.

47. Bishop Graham-Brown also made appeals on behalf of other groups, for example the Jewish Farm School, Ben Shemen, and its work. See The Jerusalem and East Mission Papers LXVII/2: Ben Shemen Children's Village, April 24, 1940.

48. See e.g., Ramsbotham, Woodhouse, and Miall, *Contemporary*, 21–30, 180–88.

49. Lang Papers, 52/137: Letter from Graham-Brown to Lang, January 21, 1937. Also in The Jerusalem and East Mission Papers LXI/2.

is situated *in the middle* and, as such, his main task is to bring those together who are involved in a violent conflict and try to find some constructive agreement on how to end it. One of the problems that a mediator has to tackle is how to break through a party's threatened psychological self-defenses. The task of a mediator is therefore, according to Curle, to be a friend. Diplomacy leading to an agreement does not necessary bring about a solution to the conflict, Curle reflects. While instead offering friendship, mutual understanding and trust are allowed to grow, something that in turn may contribute to the reduction of negative feelings and to the capacity of transforming the conflict.[50]

However, many statements in the material make it difficult to regard the Anglicans' aim of a dialogue as being built on reciprocal understanding and trust. It is obvious that the Anglicans valued their relations with other religious leaders, but, as many times before, cannot withdraw from commenting on, in their eyes, the Jewish and Muslim insufficiencies and the Christian superiority. The Anglican bishop speaks warmly about a spiritual collaboration but, at the same time, he expresses a degraded view of other religions. Bishop Graham-Brown writes to the archbishop:

> My desire is to plead and labor for the closest spiritual collaboration between Christian, Moslem and Jew, in this Holy land, believing that Islam is a degraded heresy of Christianity and that Judaism finds its completion in Christianity . . . It is not only difficult but laborious to find links of sympathy with the three. Here, if anywhere, we must achieve that friendship in its most understanding form, which Our Lord came to give; realizing that greater love hath no man than this, to give his full self for and in this friendship.[51]

Being a religious leader, the bishop even saw the possibility to act as a facilitator for moderate political forces. The bishop arranged discussions about an agreed settlement between Arabs and Jews. After a lengthy talk in Graham-Brown's study, a document was drawn up by mediators between the Jewish Agency and the Arab Higher Committee: Judah Magnes and Izzat Tannous. Graham-Brown had to do the telephoning for them and make all plans embodying oral suggestions. The bishop conveyed the message to the leaders of the Jewish Agency and the Arab Higher Committee, Moshe Shertok and the Mufti. Graham-Brown stat-

50. Curle, *Kraften*, 93–105.
51. Lang Papers 52/112: Letter from Graham-Brown to Lang, January 15, 1937.

ed in a letter to Archbishop Lang: "I am only too willing and anxious to give any help in bringing about such a meeting, and suggest that it would be of definite value to record together those points on which there was agreement concerning the situation and future of Palestine."[52]

In this case the bishop governed the situation and the context of the negotiations through providing a meeting place, doing the telephoning and helping with other practical matters. Wallensteen emphasizes the role of creating a psychological climate of cooperation between parties in conflict. Holding negotiations in secret has shown to be one component, the ability to discuss matters thoroughly another.[53] The informal nature of the bishop's actions shows that the Anglican Church was being conscious of these matters.

Thus, in the Anglican case we find examples of both advocacy and mediation. Lederach builds on Curle's work in describing conflict as a progression and elaborating the roles that emerge in the transformation of conflict from violent and destructive to constructive and peaceful manifestations.[54] Lederach notes that, according to this framework, "education, advocacy, and mediation share the goal of change and restructuring unpeaceful relationships . . . They share the vision of justice, of substantive and procedural change." The roles do differ, though. "Advocacy, for example, chooses to stand by one side for justice's sake. Mediation chooses to stand in connection to all sides for justice's sake."[55] Yet Lederach sees these roles as mutually supportive and dependent. Confrontation and advocacy can help to legitimize and articulate needs and interests of all parties in a conflict. Mediation, on the other hand, can help to reduce conflict, creating the impression of incompatibility.[56]

Also Sampson argues that the interplay of these two roles in the experience of several religious actors in conflict situations contradicts the assumption that advocacy and mediation are mutually exclusive and therefore cannot be performed by the same individual, or at least not

---

52. Lang Papers, 53/2: "Notes on discussions towards an Agreed Settlement between Arab and Jew." Enclosed document from Brown to Archbishop Lang February 10, 1938. Graham-Brown also visited Beirut together with Magnes and Tannous where they met with Palestinian leader Nuri Pasha on February 6, 1938. See also Goren, "Dissenter."

53. Wallensteen, Från krig, 295.

54. Lederach, Preparing, 13.

55. Ibid., 14–15.

56. Ibid.

concurrently.[57] In the Anglican case, however, it seems that the bishops moved in and out of advocacy and mediation roles.

BETWEEN THE PUBLIC AND PRIVATE

I started out this investigation by referring to the violent society in which the Anglican representatives lived and worked during the British Mandate period. In this context the Anglican Church made efforts to promote communication and trust among people on different levels. I have connected these efforts to the modern theories on public diplomacy in civil society. Behind these peace attempts I have found an ambivalent discourse leaning towards both Western Orientalism as well as interfaith dialogue.

The efforts made by the Anglican bishops can be connected to faith-based diplomacy. It involved interfaith worships but also advocacy for minorities and mediation through official and informal meetings for religious leaders as well as moderate political representatives. Thus, they tried in many aspects to be a facilitator for communication. I therefore regard the Anglican Church as an informal third party in civil society, working with its own means within a religious field of action. In a context where religion often was used as political tool legitimizing violence and conflicts, there were also opposing voices and counter-acts in favor of peace-building.

At the same time, the Anglican representatives in Palestine used the prayers and meetings in order to legitimize asymmetric power relations. Christian and British values often became the norms of the interpretation of the conflict, conveyed at formal meetings. The representatives of the Anglican Church, when making themselves moral authorities, conveyed a message: since the conflicting parties lived in conflict they needed moral change. The parties were morally defected but had a potential to change with help from outside. It is evident that the Anglican Church was part of Western Orientalism, British political superiority and Christian triumphalism.

In many respects this is about an interstitial "space." It has dealt with the Anglican Church as an informal "third party" trying to provide meeting places and to promote peace-building between Jews and Arabs in Palestine 1920–1948. I have discussed the role of the Anglican Church

57. Sampson "Religion," 277.

in "the civil society," which is interpreted as the part of society between the family and the state, where actions are voluntary and distinctly separate from the field of action of state authorities. Also the participation in Anglican rituals may in fact be viewed as a kind of entering into a "space in between" where people of various backgrounds could meet, connect to each other and, at best, deal with conflicts. Kaldor, illustrating this, argues that "zones of peace and zones of war exist side by side in the same territorial space."[58]

The Anglican Church in the period of study provided meeting places where friendships and human sympathy could grow. The meetings often took shape in between the formal and the informal. The informal arena could be utilized in order to test new ideas and new forms of relations. It is useful since it allows "plausible deniability." Ideas are tested privately and informally. If they do not turn out to work, one can claim they are only of private matter. If they are considered to work, however, they can be transferred to the public arena. In this way, there is a special value to meeting places in between the categories of private and public. In Palestine, during the British Mandate period, very few meeting places existed where people could meet over the borders. The Anglican Church tried to provide meeting places with joint rituals where representatives of all the religions present in Palestine could meet. The Anglican efforts may be considered as vague and insufficient, but they might nevertheless have been a first step towards better mutual understanding.

BIBLIOGRAPHY

Unpublished Sources

Lang Papers. London: Lambeth Palace Library.
The Jerusalem and East Mission (J&EM) Papers. Oxford: Middle East Centre, St Anthony's College.

Published Sources

Bible Lands, 1922 and 1937.

Encyclopedias

The Encyclopedia of Religion, New York—London, Vol. 12, 1987.

58. Kaldor, New, 138. See also Kaldor, Global.

Literature

Abu El-Assal, Riah. "The Birth and Experience of the Christian Church: The Protestant/ Anglican Perspective: Anglican Identity in the Middle East." In *Christians in the Holy Land*, edited by Michael Prior and William Taylor, 131–40. London: World of Islam Festival Trust, 1995.

Abu-Nimer, Mohammed. "Religion, Dialogue, and Non-Violent Actions in Palestinian-Israeli Conflict." *International Journal of Politics and Society* 17/3 (Spring 2004) 491–511.

Aggestam, Karin. *Reframing and Resolving Conflict: Israeli-Palestinian Negotiations 1988-1998*. Lund, Sweden: Lund University Press, 1999.

Bell, Catherine M. *Ritual Theory, Ritual Practice*. New York: Oxford University Press, 1992.

Braybrooke, Marcus. *A Wider Vision: A History of the World Congress of Faiths 1936–1996*. Oxford: Oneworld, 1996.

Chandler, David. *Bosnia: Faking Democracy after Dayton*. London: Pluto, 2000.

Cohen, Raymond. *Saving the Holy Sepulchre: How Rival Christians Came Together To Rescue Their Holiest Shrine*. Oxford: Oxford University Press, 2008.

Cragg, Kenneth. "The Anglican Church." In *Three Religions in Concord and Conflict*, edited by Arthur John Arberry, 570–95. Cambridge: Cambridge University Press, 1969.

Curle, Adam. *Kraften som förvandlar: synpunkter på ickevåld*. Stockholm: Carlsson, 1992.

Elpeleg, Zvi. *The Grand Mufti Haj Amin Al-Hussaini—Founder of the Palestinian National Movement*. London: F. Cass, 1993.

Etherington, Norman. "Missions and Empire." In *The Oxford History of the British Empire. Volume V. Historiography*, edited by Robin W. Winks, 303–14. Oxford: Oxford University Press, 1999.

Fergusson, David. *Church, State and Civil Society*. Cambridge: Cambridge University Press, 2004.

Geertz, Clifford. *The Interpretation of Cultures*. New York: Basic Books, 1973.

———. *Negara: The Theatre State in Nineteenth Century Bali*. Princeton: Princeton University Press, 1980.

Gluckman, Max. "Les rites de passage." In *Essays on the Ritual of Social Relations*, edited by Max Gluckman, 1–52. Manchester: Manchester University Press, 1975.

Gopin, Marc. *Holy War, Holy Peace: How Religion Can Bring Peace to the Middle East*. New York: Oxford University Press, 2002.

Goren, Arthur A. *"Dissenter in Zion": From the Writings of Judah L. Magnes*. Cambridge MA: Harvard University Press, 1982.

Hjärpe, Jan. "Religionshistorikern och kriget." In *Våldets Mening. Makt, minne, myt*, edited by Eva Österberg and Marie Lindstedt Cronberg, 301–7. Lund, Sweden: Nordic Academic Press, 2004.

Johnston, Douglas, ed. *Faith-Based Diplomacy: Trumping Realpolitik*. Oxford: Oxford University Press, 2008.

Kaldor, Mary. *Global Civil Society: An Answer to War*. Cambridge: Polity, 2003.

———. *New and Old Wars: Organized Violence in a Global Era*. Cambridge: Polity, 1999.

Kolinsky, Martin. *Law, Order and Riots in Mandatory Palestine, 1928-35*. Basingstoke: Macmillan, 1993.

Lederach, John Paul. *Building Peace: Sustainable Reconciliation in Divided Societies*. Washington DC: United States Institute of Peace, 1997.

———. *Preparing for Peace: Conflict Transformation Across Cultures*. Syracuse: Syracuse University Press, 1996.

Lewis, Bernard. *The Multiple Identities of the Middle East*. New York: Schocken, 2001.

Louis, Wm. Roger. "Introduction." In *The Oxford History of the British Empire: Volume IV: The Twentieth Century*, edited by Judith M. Brown and Wm. Roger Louis, 1–46. Oxford: Oxford University Press, 1999.

Marshall, Peter J. "The History of the Empire: 1918 to the 1960s: Keeping Afloat." In *The Cambridge Illustrated History of the British Empire*, edited by Peter J. Marshall, 80–106. Cambridge: Cambridge University Press, 1996.

Mattar, Philip. *The Mufti of Jerusalem: Al-Hajj Amin al-Husayni and the Palestinian National Movement*. New York: Columbia University Press, 1988.

Morris, Benny. *Righteous Victims: A History of the Zionist-Arab Conflict 1899–1999*. London: John Murrey, 2000.

Murphy, Raymond. *Social Closure: The Theory of Monopolization and Exclusion*. Oxford: Clarendon, 1988.

Okkenhaug, Inger Marie. *Gender, Race and Religion: Nordic Missions, 1860–1940*. Uppsala: Swedish Institute for Mission Studies, 2003.

———. *The Quality of Heroic Living, of High Endeavour and Adventure: Anglican Mission, Women and Education in Palestine, 1888–1948*. Bergen: Bergen University, 1999.

Owen, Nicholas. "Critics of Empire in Britain." In *The Oxford History of the British Empire: Volume IV: The Twentieth Century*, edited by Judith M. Brown and Wm. Roger Louis, 188–211. Oxford: Oxford University Press, 1999.

Paris, Roland. *At War's End: Building Peace after Civil Conflict*. Cambridge: Cambridge University Press, 2004.

Porter, Andrew. "Empires in the Mind." In *The Cambridge Illustrated History of the British Empire*, edited by P. J. Marshall, 185–223. Cambridge: Cambridge University Press, 1996.

Putnam, Robert D. *Bowling Alone: The Collapse and Revival of American Community*. London: Simon & Schuster, 2001.

Putnam, Robert D., Robert Leonardi, and Raffaella Y. Nanetti. *Making Democracy Work: Civic Traditions in Modern Italy*. Princeton: Princeton University Press, 1992.

Ramsbotham, Oliver, Tom Woodhouse, and Hugh Miall. *Contemporary Conflict Resolution: The Prevention, Management and Transformation of Deadly Conflicts*. Cambridge: Polity, 2011.

Said, Edward W. *Orientalism*. London: Routledge, 1978.

Sampson, Cynthia. "Religion and Peacebuilding." In *Peacemaking in International Conflict: Methods and Techniques*, edited by I. William Zartman and J. Lewis Rasmussen, 273–321. Washington DC: United States Institute of Peace, 2003.

Scheffler, Thomas. "Interfaith Dialogue and Cultural Diplomacy." Paper presented at DAVO (Deutsch Arbeitsgemeinschaft Vordere Orient), Hamburg, 2003. Online: www2.uibk.ac.at/forschung/weltordnung/scheffler_dialogue_and_diplomacy.pdf.

Sela, Avraham. "The 'Wailing Wall' Riots (1929) as a Watershed in the Palestine Conflict." *The Muslim World* 84/1-2, (January-April 1994) 60–94.

Shepherd, Naomi. *Ploughing Sand: British Rule in Palestine 1917–1948*. London: John Murray, 1999.

———. *The Zealous Intruders: The Western Rediscovery of Palestine.* London: William Collins, 1987.

Småberg, Maria. *Ambivalent Friendship: Anglican Conflict Handling and Education for Peace in Jerusalem 1920–1948.* Lund, Sweden: Lund University Press, 2005.

Smith, Charles D. *Palestine and the Arab-Israeli Conflict.* Boston: Bedford/St Martin's, 2007.

Smock, David R. *Interfaith Dialogue and Peacebuilding.* Washington DC: United States Institute of Peace, 2002.

———. *Religious Contributions to Peacemaking: When Religion Brings Peace, Not War.* Washington DC: United States Institute of Peace, 2006.

Stanley, Brian. *The Bible and the Flag. Protestant Missions and British Imperialism in the Nineteenth and Twentieth Centuries.* Leicester: Apollos, 1990.

Stillman, Norman A. *The Jews of Arab Lands: A History and Source Book.* Philadelphia: Jewish Publication Society of America, 1979.

Tejirian, Eleanor H. "Faith of Our Fathers: Near East Relief and the Near East Foundation—From Mission to NGO." Paper presented at the conference "Altruism and Imperialism: The Western Religious and Cultural Missionary Enterprise in the Middle East," Middle East Institute, Bellagio, Italy, August 2000. Online: http://www.ciaonet.org/conf/mei01/poa01.html.

Tsimhoni, Daphne. *Christian Communities in Jerusalem and the West Bank since 1948.* Westport, CT: Praeger, 1993.

———. "The Status of the Arab Christians under the British Mandate in Palestine." *Middle Eastern Studies* 2/4 (1984) 166–192.

Wallensteen, Peter. *Från krig till fred. Om konfliktlösning i det globala systemet.* Stockholm: Almqvist & Wiksell, 1994.

Washbrook, D. A. "Orients and Occidents: Colonial Discourse Theory and the Historiography of the British Empire." In *The Oxford History of the British Empire: Volume V: Historiography,* edited by Robin W. Winks, 596–611. Oxford: Oxford University Press, 1999.

Wasserstein, Bernard. *The British in Palestine: The Mandatory Government and the Arab-Jewish Conflict 1917–1929.* Oxford: Blackwell, 1991.

———. *Divided Jerusalem: The Struggle for the Holy City.* London: Profile, 2001.

8

Linking War and Religion

Some Observations

KJELL-ÅKE NORDQUIST

It was for a long time an outmoded question to ask if and how "religion" and "war" could be linked theoretically in a meaningful way. Wasn't the relation between religion and war a matter that Europe settled already in 1648? And, if not, didn't modernization theory in the 1800s solve the matter once and for all? Modernization theory predicted that religion should fade away from public life, when rationalism, individualism, capitalism, and secularism take root and is spread over the world. Secularization meant that religion leaves the public sphere and, if it survives at all, stays with the private. As a consequence, religion will also leave the position as the dominating, conventional worldview and become relegated to an increasingly odd position and perspective on life, if not disappearing completely.

This view of the consequences of modernization is a standard introduction in studies on religion and war during the last decade. It focuses one of the most unquestioned predictions that Durkheim, Comte, Weber, Marx, Freud, and others left—in various forms—for posterity to deal with. Pretty much throughout the twentieth century it was an unquestioned assumption in philosophy and the social sciences.

However, at one point, indications contrary to the modernists' "fading-away hypothesis" became too many to be defensible. While religion became increasingly associated with ethnic conflict from the early 1980s and onwards,[1] there was a lack of explanations to this. This devel-

---

1. Fox, *Religion, Civilization, and Civil War*, 125.

opment had a double effect. It was not only a break with the predictions of modernization theory, but also a challenge to the *realist* paradigm, with its focus on material interests and power, as against ideas and other "soft" dimensions of life (which religions often represent).

At that point, to what extent was it necessary to redefine also fundamental assumptions about the global system as seen during the twentieth century?

NEW CONFLICTS MAKE A NEW WORLD ORDER?

The discrepancy between theory and reality—with respect to religion and war—was not possible to settle by changed operationalizations or methodological approaches. It became too evident, that while the number of conflicts increased significantly for a few years in the wake of the control exerted by the two Cold War superpowers on Third World governments,[2] a new perspective, a substantially reformed, or new, theory (replacing *realism*) was needed in order to explain how ethnicity, nationalism, and religion, often in combination, became significant reasons for contention, conflict, and armed confrontations.

One author, Francis Fukuyama, proclaimed in 1992 the end of history—there will be no more major ideological strides, instead liberal democracy will dominate for the rest of human history.[3] As a reaction to this view, Samuel P. Huntington argued the year after, that there is after the Cold War a new and major visible division on a global level that will shape the future, namely that between civilizations, including their religions. He predicted clashes of civilizations to come, not necessarily in one moment but in many local and regional conflicts. He was widely criticized, for simplifying and overlooking cross-civilization cooperation, peace agreements, and the fact that most conflicts are not explained by civilization lines.[4] But Huntington argues that his view is about the future, not history. "Faith and family, blood and belief, are what people identify with and what they will fight and die for" Huntington concludes in a response to his critics.[5]

2. From forty-three armed conflicts in 1989 to fifty-three in 1992. See Themnér and Wallensteen, "Armed Conflict, 1946–2010," 527.

3. Fukuyama, *The End of History*.

4. See for instance Russett et al, "Clash of Civilizations," and Fox, *Religion, Civilization, and Civil War*, 205.

5. Huntington, "If Not Civilizations What?"

But Huntington, a political scientist himself, did not convince his colleagues. In particular since his predictions were not supported by actual developments.[6] The classic view of the international system, *realism*, has its basis in materialism (the national interest) and anarchy (no global monopoly of violence). Eva Bellin, when reviewing religion and war studies, points at international security scholars who take cultural variables into their assessment even if they "would resist the argument that cultural variables can trump material interest and structural imperatives."[7] When referring to Barnett, for instance, Bellin finds that "a realist model can integrate a causal role of ideational forces like religion in international politics."[8] Also *liberalism*, with its criticism of the realists' lack of interest in norms and institutions, is open for including the role religion can play in this regard. Bellin concludes that it is better to "abandon the endless prosecution of "paradigm wars," move beyond commonsense observations that *religion matters* in international politics, and explore the truly challenging theoretical question: when does religion matter and *how*?"[9]

Bellin's advice brings us back to our starting point: how can religion be linked to conflict and war? In order to answer this question, we need to know what the situation looks like.

A CHANGING PICTURE

Different events are used by different authors to mark a symbolic breaking point for the shift between the old realist perspective, marked by the Cold War and basically blind for ideas, including religions, and a new (not yet satisfactorily named) one. When did the change take place?

Some would focus on Ayatollah Khomeini's takeover in Iran in 1979—already ten years before the ending of the Cold War. Other observers note the increase in internal and ethnically driven armed conflicts in the 1990s, after the end of the Cold War, something that resulted in a record number—fifty-three—of such conflicts in 1993.[10] A third

6. Fox concludes that there is "little support for any of Huntington's predictions" when analyzing (changes of) conflict patterns from the Cold war and post-Cold war era, up to 2000. See Fox, *Religion, Civilization, and Civil War*, 205.

7. Bellin, "Faith in Politics," 340.

8. Ibid., 341.

9. Ibid., 341f., Bellin's italics.

10. Themnér and Wallensteen, "Armed Conflict, 1946–2010," 527.

observer would begin in 2001 and put 9/11 as the sign for a profound change of our understanding of the relationship between religion and war.

These three starting points do not exclude each other. Instead they are informative beginnings of an on-going analysis of religion and war. By focusing different aspects—religion, ethnicity, suicide terrorism— they illustrate the diversity of issues which characterize both research and the general debate on this matter until today.

The religious dimension entered this debate not from the perspective of established, protracted conflicts—such as those in Kashmir, Palestine or Colombia—but through spectacular events, maybe inspiring each other in some cases, but not systematically coordinated.

During the 1990s, there was a series of conspicuous, religiously framed terrorist attacks—from the 1993 al Qaeda attempt on New York World Trade Center, the 1995 U.S. Christian Patriot Movement Oklahoma Federal Office bombing, the U.S. Embassy bombings in Kenya and Tanzania in 1998, and to the 9/11 attack in 2001. These events gained a media and political interest that put the more structurally dependent development beginning in the end of the same decade (of reduced armed conflicts) in the shade. Impressions of increased violence in a religiously dominated world of conflicts gained footing instead.

The general pattern of armed conflict after the end of the Second World War illustrates an increase both in the number of conflicts and independent states—the last major addition to the list of independent states came with the break-up of the Soviet Union. Obviously, some kind of relationship exists between the number of states, and the number of conflicts, but that observation is basically trivial. There is no given relationship between the two: more states can have less number of conflicts and many conflicts can take place within just one state, at a given point in time. The pattern is much more complex and interesting. Other reasons—then just many potential conflict parties such as states—need to be found if we shall understand fluctuations in the number, character, and intensity of armed conflicts over time. During the Cold War, superpower rivalry—often materializing through proxy states—together with systemic characteristics that caused escalation and arms race, were investigated as possible explanations.[11] Over the global polarization at the time presided the two political systems, capitalism and communism.

11. Vasquez, "The Steps to War."

During the Cold War it was not possible to identify clear-cut chains of causes and effects, beginning with one of the two ideologies, and ending up as an explanation of the start of a specific armed conflict or war. In some current debates, religion has taken over the position of capitalism or communism, as a short-cut explanation for global conflict.

But "religion" is a concept cross-cutting both "capitalism," "communism," as well as "civilization." With Christianity expanding widely in Africa and Latin America, with a European Muslim identity developing, and with a general globalization of religious beliefs, regionally defined versions of traditional, major belief systems establish themselves in what is, for a given religion, geographically new areas. Civilizations are likely to be gradually molded in new forms as generations come. Most likely, this makes Huntington's thesis even less attractive.

Religion is as vague and widespread a social phenomenon as ever was, or is, capitalism or communism. In addition, "religion" is a wider, and therefore different phenomenon in relation to "ideology." Both capitalists and communists have historically found ways to embrace the same religion, so introducing "religion," or "civilization," as an independent variable, is likely to cause even more (theoretical and empirical) problems, for understanding conflict in the future.

SOME FIGURES

This author made for the year 1989 a descriptive measurement of "religious involvement"[12] in ongoing major armed conflicts. Focus was on the locations (countries most often) where either an international or civil conflict took place. Civil wars were either about territory (state-formation conflicts) or about government control (civil war). A state, such as India, can have more than one such conflict (dyadic), but is here counted as only one location.

1989 is the year of the ending of the Cold War, on-going conflicts in that year therefore reflect a Cold War situation. During the twenty year period since then, the number of armed conflicts went from forty-three in 1989, to fifty-three in 1992, and were from there decreasing to thirty-

---

12. Religious involvement is a situation where (1) at least one party refers to a religious body of thinking for legitimizing a constitution or conflict behavior, and/or (2) the polarization of parties is underpinned primarily by religious identity and/or theological perspectives. Nordquist, "Religion and Armed Conflict," 48.

six in 2009 and to thirty in 2010.[13] This rainbow-formed track over the two decades 1989–2009 includes a large number of ethnically motivated conflicts in the wake of the Cold War, including the break up of former Yugoslavia. Also a large number of peace agreements were signed in this period, often with the assistance of the UN or other international actors.

The following table gives the figures for the location (country) of armed conflicts with religious involvement in 1989 and 2010, respectively.

Location of Armed Conflict with Religious
Involvement in 1989 and 2010, respectively

	Involvement of Religion			
	1989		2010	
Type of Conflict	Yes	No	Yes	No
Government	3	14	11	8
Territory	6	8	3	4
	Σ 31		Σ 26	

What is interesting in the comparison above is not the figures as such, but the change in proportions. During the two decades, religious involvement in armed conflicts has increased in conflicts over government, that is, conflicts that challenge the incumbent government. Conflict over territory challenge the constitutional structure of a state, up to the level of secession, but this is a clear minority of the cases. As a share of those locations which experience conflict during the whole period we have seen an increase in religious involvement of at least one party over that period.

Given this picture and what a table like this tells is, that the claims, behavior, and expressed motivations for violent action (by at least one of the parties) are dressed in a language referring to religious texts. We cannot always measure how serious, or convinced, a given actor might be, but for the sake of our investigation, it is enough to observe manifest, violent behavior.

While the figures of armed conflict are currently the lowest since the 1970s, the general impression is nevertheless to the contrary, i.e.,

13. Pettersson and Themnér, *States in Armed Conflict*, 2010.

that conflicts are on the rise, the world is increasingly less secure, and that unpredictable forces—such as ethnic identity, religion, and by them inspired suicide bombers—are primary reasons behind ongoing conflicts. The picture of armed conflicts is increasingly fragmented.

"WAR"—ARMED STRUGGLE AND SYMBOL

When authors state that religion is a "cause of war," or that religion instigates or mobilizes for war, the statement is often meant as a general observation: it is believed to be "true" even if it is not put in distinct terms. Or put differently, it is acceptable that the statement needs an interpretation that makes sense both to the concepts of "religion" and of "war" themselves, and to their assumed relationship.

There are several ways of understanding "war," independently or in relation to "terrorism." Let's look at three types, relevant for our analysis: a legal, scientific, and a "fanatic"[14] version. All these can, in addition, be related to the justification of war, either in relation to the initiation of war—*jus ad bellum*—or the conduct of war—*jus in bello*.

It was, for instance, a catching expression when President George W. Bush declared "war on terror" on September 20, 2001, but when said by a president in a context of an emerging conflict scenario, it also raised issues from a legal and political point of view: was this something more than a symbolic talk about a country's commitment to fight terrorism in all its manifestations? Was it a new type of state response to hostile behavior? The President exemplified, in the same speech, that his intention was directed towards terror organizations, when saying that "our war on terror begins with al Qaeda, but it does not end there. It will not end until every terrorist group of global reach has been found, stopped, and defeated."[15]

"Terror" is a violent tactic that has been used since historic times by individuals, groups and states for different purposes. "Terror" is also a feeling that humans can experience in particular situations. A question raised by "war on terror" is, among other, if this type of war is comparable to what international law would call an "international armed attack," or for that matter an "internal armed attack"? Lawyers have since

14. "Fanatic" stands here for simplified and overstated, beyond concrete points of reference.

15. Bush, *Speech to a Joint Session*.

2001 discussed, for instance, if "actions against al Qaeda are deemed to be part of an armed conflict under international law"[16] or if attacks by organizations, such as al Qaeda, are meeting the criteria for self-defense according to the UN Charter (articles 2 and 51) or not.[17]

According to Natasha Balendra, "many commentators maintain that the conflict with al Qaeda is not an armed conflict, international or non-international."[18] The arguments applied are that al Qaeda is not a state actor (international armed conflict) plus that its activities are not taking place in one but in different geographic locations (non-international armed conflict) and are organized by cells that have not reached a level of organization and command structure envisaged by Common Article 3 of the Geneva Conventions.[19] On the other hand, some commentators would give the Common Article 3 such a broad scope that it is applicable in "any armed conflict that is not an international armed conflict"[20] and therefore Balendra concludes that it is "difficult to decide whether to characterize the conflict as an international armed conflict, a non-international armed conflict, or some hybrid of the two."[21]

This discussion is of value to our reflections since it elaborates a number of dimensions of armed conflict that indicate the complexity of the phenomenon. Also, we will have reason to return to this perspective later, when considering the consequences of fundamentalist actions in the name of religion.

Social scientists have for decades tried to give war and armed conflict an analytically effective definition, that is, one that produces valid and consistent identifications of the same phenomenon. A widely used definition among social scientists departs from the intensity of certain behavior to identify an armed conflict, and states that an "interstate armed conflict occurs between two or more states" and an "intrastate armed conflict occurs between the government of a state and internal opposition groups." In both cases, the conflict is at all reported if there are twenty-five battle-related deaths per year or more, and it is called "minor" if this number is fewer than one thousand, and "war" if at

16. Balendra, "Defining Armed Conflict," 2463.
17. Heinze, "The Evolution of International Law."
18. Balendra, "Defining Armed Conflict," 2472.
19. Ibid., 2469f.
20. Ibid., 2474.
21. Ibid.

least one thousand battle-related deaths are reported in a year.[22] This definition can be used both for identifying single cases for qualitative studies and for quantitative research, and is for instance the basis for the Uppsala Conflict Data Program (UCDP). In addition, UCDP differentiates between conflicts over government and conflicts over territory, where the latter are conflicts that challenge the present constitutional structure of a state.

Departing from the Geneva Conventions' focus on state actors and non-state actors, the UCDP definition adds intensity and, although roughly, a content variable (government or territory). Even so, many situations that are considered as "conflicts" (or community violence, disturbances, riots, revolutions, upheavals and the like), are not included by such definitions. UCDP has therefore developed data on one-sided violence, as well as conflict between non-state actors.

THE JUSTIFIED WAR

"War" is a concept that indicates an activity that needs moral justification. To start war is not a trivial decision. The existential dimension of war, and of violence, puts these concepts in need of justifications that go beyond what citizens normally include in daily negotiations and considerations. The religious formalization of such considerations are in Judaism, Christianity, and Islam, formulated in what has been called just war traditions. Within Buddhism, with Sri Lanka as a useful example, just war type of approaches to the realities of violence and state interest have as well been developed.[23] Also within Confucianism, principles for war in a non-ideal world have been developed both historically and in contemporary debate.[24]

These ways of thinking among religious leaders and thinkers, indicate a profound need to regulate war and doing so through identifying what is morally justifiable. Critics may argue that these traditions are not limiting war, or behavior in wartime, but rather give acceptance to war as an idea, and to certain war behavior.

For the three Abrahamic traditions mentioned above, and in light of the on-going debate on conflictual relationships between these three

---

22. Petterson and Themnér, *States in Armed Conflict*, 29.

23. See for instance Bartolomeusz, *In Defense of Dharma*.

24. See Bell, *Beyond Liberal Democracy*.

religions, there are maybe surprisingly similar arguments and perspectives within them, on how they approach the ethical challenges of going to war in the first place, and if so, how to conduct war.[25] These norms do not avert violence in the name of religion, and they were not made for that purpose either. Instead, these systems of thought have survived a number of military and technological developments, and thereby proved both flexibility and, it must be admitted, a lack of consistency, over more than a millennium-long period. The international legal system has during the last two centuries formulated norms in this field, and eventually developed a framework of law that actually gives less practical room for what can be considered *jus ad bellum*, than does, for instance, the Christian Just War tradition. It is "easier" today, to justify war on moral grounds within a Christian just war tradition, than it is from an international legal perspective.[26]

"War" is one of the most challenging, and if justified, mobilizing concepts on the societal level that exist. When war is approaching a society it is a call for unity, sacrifice, and preparedness. Therefore, a convincingly justified war becomes a supreme rallying tool for any leader.

Militant religious groups, who are close to or do practice selective killing and terrorism such as Christian right-wing groups in the U.S., like the Christian Identity and American Patriot movements, would use the concept of "war" when describing their necessary mission in this world. This kind of war, according to Mark Juergensmeyer, can be described as a "cosmic war," a war that evokes a global spiritual confrontation, beyond the worldly in-fighting of "regular" wars. Cosmic wars release the wrath of the heavens towards the evil of this world.[27] This kind of war is a grand scenario, once and for all sorting out the struggle between the good and bad, the saved and the sinners.

TERRORISM AND WAR

Theoretically speaking, a war includes among other things *actors* and *issues*. In real life, wars have been between at least two parties, sometimes more, who have been fighting for their issues while at the same time they have been able to identify each other and act against each other

25. Nordquist, *Contradicting Peace Proposals in the Palestine Conflict*, chapter 6.
26. Nordquist, *From Just War to Justified Intervention*, 73.
27. Juergensmeyer, *Terror in the Mind of God*, 49f.

in an exchange of a destructive nature, often called "conflict behavior." Sometimes a stalemate has occurred, but even if it has taken years to overcome such a situation, the parties have not lost track of the other side.

It is a different situation, though, if actions—even if portrayed as "war"—take place with years in between instances of "conflict behavior" and between hardly identifiable actors? Is it still "war," one may ask, comparable to what we normally refer to as "war"?

One typical aspect of a terrorist act is the avoidance of direct confrontation with the enemy. This is contrary to the conventional understanding of "war." What is analytically problematic is not so much that the terrorist is involved in an act where there is no room for compromise—which parties in traditional wars are often prepared to—as the fact that the situation is not one of war at all, in the sense of two parties fighting each other militarily. War, we have seen, is a relation between (at least) two enemies, but for the terrorist in order to achieve the goal of terror, direct contact with the enemy is avoided. A unilateral surprise attack is produced. This is what causes terror, fear. Such an attack, which Juergensmeyer shows well, can be both effective in itself, and performative, by impacting on indirectly upon individuals that happen to be present or become aware of the event later.[28]

Terrorism is in this way different also from guerilla tactics. Guerilla movements, with their fish-in-the-water tactic and typically asymmetric capacity in relation to government armies, do not always avoid direct confrontation with these armies. In a specific situation a guerilla army can very well be as strong as a state army.

For this reason, the use of the "war" concept in relation to any "single party events"—even if they are terror actions—can only be relevant on a symbolic level. But when used for analytical purposes, it easily leads to confusion since: very different events are brought together, as if they share more qualities than they actually do.

As a consequence, and on a wider note, it also means that acts of "terror" are incorporated into a paradigm, a language of analysis, which introduces a discussion on terrorism in the light of dimensions such as strategy, escalation, damage, justification, and ending. Besides justification, this is not a moral issue, it is still a scientific one, but it begs for restraint. Concepts like these, developed for well-defined structural con-

28. Ibid.

ditions, are simply not likely to be applicable for situations where these conditions are not at hand.

In this author's view, this leads the analysis away from comparability with other conflict situations. It also leads the analysis away from identifying possibilities to counteract terrorism through other than military approaches.

WHAT IS "RELIGION"?

Although religions have existed since "time immemorial," it doesn't follow that "religion" since then has been identified and conceived of as distinct from for instance "secular," as is done in a modern society. This may sound tricky for someone who takes for granted, for instance, separation between religion and politics. If religion is seamlessly integrated with the world in which "we live and move and have our being,"[29] it disappears as a concept for something separate and distinct—a prerequisite for any meaningful comparison of a phenomenon. It is well known that Islam does not on a dogmatic level accept a distinction in life between what, from another perspective, could be called the secular and the religious. Whether Christianity does this distinction on a dogmatic level depends for instance on how the word of Jesus is interpreted when he, responding to a question of taxes, states that one should render unto Caesar the things which are Caesar's, and unto God the things that are God's.[30] The question is open.

Historians of religion, when studying religious phenomena and behavior on a global level under the assumption that these phenomena share something in common have often formulated a definition of religion like the one by James B. Pratt in the 1920s, where religion is "a serious and social attitude of individuals or groups towards the power or those powers which they consider as ultimately controlling their interests and destinies."[31]

Some modern historians of religion would however be so cautious that they would preferably abstain from any definition at all. Here, the discussion goes in two directions, one focusing the linguistic and cultural context which any Western scholar has to deal with, and the other

29. Epimenides, Cretan philosopher, quoted in Acts 17.

30. See Matthew 22.

31. James B. Pratt, 1922, quoted in Ringgren and Ström, *Religionerna i historia och nutid*, 7 (author's translation).

focusing on the impossibility of giving essentialist definitions at all. For instance, Winston L. King finds that:

> The very attempt to define *religion*, to find some distinctive or possibly unique or set of qualities that distinguish the "religious" from the remainder of human life, is primarily a Western concern. The attempt is a natural consequence of the Western speculative, intellectualistic, and scientific disposition. It is also the product of the dominant Western religious mode, what is called the Judeo-Christian climate, or more accurately, the theistic inheritance from Judaism, Christianity, and Islam . . . Even Western thinkers who recognize their cultural bias find it hard to escape, because the assumptions of theism permeate the linguistic structures that shape their thought . . . Many practical and conceptual difficulties arise when one attempts to apply such a dichotomous pattern across the board to all cultures.[32]

Given a respect for differences between cultures, and the fact that Western philosophy and culture is just one among many, King refrains in the quote above from developing a definition that by the very idea of being generalizable asks a question that not all are prepared for, or even interested in, responding to.

If we accept the division of reality into a secular and religious part arises for practical reasons a need for different, and pragmatic, definitions of religion. The scholarly community tend to group around, at least, four types of definitions: *substantive* (what content makes religion unique?), *functional* (which role does religion play for individual and society?), *verstehende* (how can a religious situation be understood from within?), and *formal* (which traits bring religious characteristics together?).[33]

In an interesting way, Eric O. Hanson makes a link between the specific features of religion and politics, respectively, in order to reach an analytical interface between the two.[34] He departs from the role both of them require: *observation* on part of those involved, and *judgment* on part of the system. Hanson's table summarizes this link in the following way:

32. King, "Religion," 284 (italics original).
33. Blasi, "Definition of Religion," 129.
34. Hanson, *Religion and Politics*, 76.

The Relationship between Religion and Politics

Religion	Politics
Observation	
"pattern of beliefs and activities that expresses ultimate meaning in a person's life and death"	"pattern of beliefs and activities that determines who gets what, when, how" plus "who gets to participate"
Judgment	
"pattern of beliefs and activities that predispose and accompany the person's contact with the Other in which one accepts one's inmost self"	"pattern of beliefs and activities in which rightly constituted authority exercises legitimate coercion for the common good"

In this way Hanson tries to create a structural similarity between the two fields—politics and religion.[35]

The vague, or wide, coverage of content that is included by such broad definitions of religion makes them highly problematic for meaningful comparison or theory-building—for instance what could it mean if we talk about a "religious war" with this kind of definition of "religion"?

CRITICS IN THE DEBATE

Critics in the current debate may not always focus on the theoretical problem of linking "war" and "religion" as concepts, but would accept doing so while at the same time focus on other aspects of the problem. For instance, that in debates on religion and war, it easily becomes an assumption that what is seen is what is there to see. If the relationship between religion and war is discussed on a general note, few would identify those *religiously* motivated governments that refrain from mixing religion and politics as part of a peace-making role of religion, for instance.

Another critical perspective, on the most general level, is that since religions are capable to include seemingly diametrically opposite positions, it is never a sufficient level of investigation to stay with "religious affiliation" as an indicator of anything, basically. Pacifists and war-

---

35. Harold Lasswell's classical definition of politics, from 1936, has inspired Hanson.

mongers, communists and capitalists, cultural relativists and ethnocen-
trists—all can adhere to the same religion on a certain level of a religious
community.

There are also those scholars who criticize research on the connection between religion and war, again not by rejecting the connection between the two as such, but by challenging the methodological
approaches—often quantitative—taken by other scholars and their approaches' capacity to produce tenable conclusions.

William T. Cavanaugh argues in his study on secular ideology and
roots of modern conflict that it was part of the creation of modernity
itself to introduce the idea of a division between what was "religion"
and what is "secular."[36] The Thirty Years' War in Europe, for that very
reason, was not over religious loyalties according to Cavanaugh, but
over enforcing the state as an institution, against a (Catholic) Church
that historically was in control of fundamental power aspirations of state
leaders, such as the right to initiate war. Having analyzed the links and
alliances between European leaders right after 1648, Cavanaugh finds
no evidence of new bonds or a concentration of religion-based links
between states as a consequence of the Thirty Years' War. There was
the same criss-cross over religious borders, explained rather by state-
building alliance formations than religion. The peace of Westphalia
in 1648 made the European state stronger as an institution, but didn't
bring the two allegedly fighting Christian traditions (Catholicism and
Protestantism) into alliances against each other, neither during the war
nor in years to come. As an illustration, Cavanaugh quotes the Swedish
chancellor Axel Oxenstierna, architect of the Swedish intervention in
the Thirty Years' War, who stated that the war was "not so much a matter
of religion, but rather of saving the *status publicus*, wherein religion is
also comprehended."[37]

While Cavanaugh looks into a particular period and tries to gather
case by case information on religion and alliances, Gerard Powers looks
at quantitative studies on modern cases of connections between religion
and war. His conclusion is that "these studies offer useful aggregate in-
dicators of the incidence of and trends in the religious dimensions of
conflicts, but they must be complemented with a much more sophisticated qualitative understanding of the role of religion." Powers notes that

36. Cavanaugh, *The Myth of Religious Violence*.
37. Quoted in Cavanaugh, *The Myth of Religious Violence*, 160.

such studies overlook the intensity of beliefs, as well as the interaction between religious identity and "ethnic, national, racial, class, cultural, gender, and political identities."[38] Powers has more ambitious questions than quantitative studies hitherto have been able to respond to. And he may be right as well—some issues are simply not possible to probe on quantitative terms.

A second aspect that concerns Powers is that quantitative studies have a "monolithic, undifferentiated, and functionalist approach to religion"[39] which often fails to understand the differences within religions—differences that can be as significant as differences between religions.

Some authors have tried to reach beyond this argument, and include qualitative aspects of religions in relation to war. Isak Svensson looks, in his study of religion and conflict resolution in civil wars,[40] into the demands formulated by parties in conflict. His interested was whether conflicts involving religion are more intractable than other. One of his findings is, that religious dissimiliarities do not make the parties less likely to reach a negotiated agreement. He also finds, that religious incompatibilities, in comparison to ethnic differences, seems to be a factor that makes a settlement less likely. Finally, also Svensson finds that Huntington's thesis, discussed above, does not get supported for the period that was studied. Arguing against Huntington's hypothesis, Svensson claims that "conflicts with participants from different religious traditions (civilizations) are not less likely to be peacefully settled through negotiations."[41]

EXTREME CONFLICTS IN A MORE PEACEFUL WORLD?

While conflict of a traditional nature—like civil wars and interstate wars—have been reduced on the whole the last two decades, we have seen at the same time how new conflict behavior (terror acts and suicide terrorism) is growing in number. Such acts have for long been mainly associated with ethnic or nationalist struggles in the Third World, and sometimes with a religious argument included—for instance by Tamil

38. Powers, "Religion and Peacebuilding," 320.
39. Ibid.
40. Svensson, "Fighting with Faith."
41. Ibid., 943.

or Palestinian groups. Terrorism and suicidal acts was one of many tactics. During the Cold War this was with a few exceptions a non-Western phenomenon. This kind of attacks were not in Western media addressed as "new types of wars", or for that matter particularly devastating, or altering relations between cultures or civilizations, even if they had religious pretexts. After the spectacular events in the 1990s, identified in the introduction of this article, the situation has changed, in the eyes of the West. The question was: is this war? Or is it something which we haven't yet given a proper name?

If extended beyond recognition, the concept of "war" puts itself at a distance from this new reality. By employing concepts of war, from media or even from the terrorists themselves, rather than developing new analytical descriptions that cover all morally reasonable dimensions (including from a criminal, psychological, and sociological perspectives)—or maybe formulating hybrid concepts as Balendra mentions above—it becomes even more difficult to see the relationship between these acts and, for instance, "religion"—or something else.

By stretching "war," confusion is created also around "terrorism"—which is a phenomenon that has vague analytical resemblances with "war" or "armed conflict." Currently there is a conceptual unclarity which creates anaytical problems and problems on the level of media and social psychology—the world seems less safe on the surface than it was during the Cold War, which—due to established concepts and a language to deal with its crises—in comparison appears to have been a stable, predictable and basically more peaceful situation.

EXTREME RELIGIONS IN A SECULARIZING WORLD?

Somewhat similar is the situation regarding how religions become key aspects of conflict in the beginning of this millennium: in a clear way since the 1980s and, according to Jonathan Fox, with an increasing presence in conflicts of different kind—ethnoreligious, ethnic, nationalist, and the like.[42] The politicization of religion in these situations allows religions to be expressed as a mobilizing and justifying tool for religious and secular leaders alike.

Secularization has not spread globally with the introduction of modern lifestyles, as we have previously noted. In periods of economic

---

42. Fox, *Religion, Civilization, and Civil War.*

decline, religion has instead returned as a domestic, political explanation for the failure of governments with secular development oriented policies in some Third World countries, such as the Philippines and Algeria.

To summarize: While there is a conflict pattern emerging on the fringes of traditional conflict behavior—such as that of suicide terrorism—there is also an emerging language on the fringes of religion—in the form of what was previously called "fanatic" interpretations.

It would be easy to associate these two trends with each other, but that is countered to some extent by the fact that there are fanatics that do not propose others or themselves to go suicidal in their actions, and there are as well nonreligious suicide attacks. How should a nettle be constructed in order to grasp the religious dimension in such a situation?

IS THERE A CRITICAL FACTOR?

We assume that pacifists don't justify or start war. From a similar way of thinking—the parallel is however not perfect—it should not be a surprise if fanatic and violence-prone interpreters of holy texts—of any religion—in the end will either justify a specific deadly act or even orchestrate it. It is not particularly challenging to identify or even understand how such a chain of events can unfold. It is almost a circular process: what is justified is performed, and what is performed shows faithfulness, and faithfulness is justified.

The challenge for research comes in understanding how religions that include *both* violent and nonviolent imagery, and *both* justifying and non-justifying views on a particular matter, and from that dual point of departure become tools for one or the other position. When religion is an open source for any preferred view—what is it then, that decides the outcome of the use of religion? This is, according to this author, where the answer to Bellin's question above, begins.

Some readers may remember the emerging quantitative approach to studies of causes of war during the last part of the past century. One famous project at the time was called the Correlates of War Project.[43] We can draw a parallel in scientific development to current attempts today at identifying critical variables on the relationship between religion and war. Interestingly, in the search for causes of war in the past century, the researchers were looking at characteristics of the system of states, and found factors explaining *peace* rather than war. This finding was, briefly

43. Vasquez, "The Steps to War."

stated, that democratic states don't fight each other. Very few, if any, deviation from this pattern can be identified for long historic periods of time. It holds over time, and in a large variety of situations, in wartime as well as peace.[44]

One working hypothesis would be, given this experience from causes of war research, that similar types of information about the nature of religions, and about their position with regard to principles and perspectives on themselves and other groups, can be a useful addition to our knowledge about what makes religion a tool for war.

WHERE TO LOOK FOR EXPLANATIONS?

Assuming the most difficult case of religious conflict is between different religions, let's make the experiment and ask what characterizes a religion that is likely to stay out of armed conflict when dealing with other religions, but also with the society as whole?

Democratic states have the choice to initiate war, or stay out, also in their relations with other democratic states. For some reason they consistently stay out. It is still an open question how to explain this in detail. Without going into this discussion too far, three types of explanations are often presented: accountability (leaders who start war will not be reelected), norms (democratically minded peoples are less violent), and state preferences (states with the same institutional preferences are less likely to get into violent conflict).[45]

There are two dimensions which contain aspects that have structural similarities to these explanations of the democratic peace, and who are intersting to discuss in relation to religions.

Let's be basic. If we take as a point of departure the very nature of a social conflict we find a *relationship*. Without relations, no conflict. Certainly, war is a relation, often intensive and destructive, between at least two actors.

Any religion, or ideology, can adopt one out of two fundamentally different ways of relating to the rest of the world, or to a specific counterparty— it can develop an attitude and behavior of *exposition* or *imposition*. A believer can either practice one's views and beliefs in full respect both of oneself and of the other religion(s), but without propos-

44. Lektzian and Souva, "A Comparative Theory Test."
45. Ibid.

ing anyone else to convert or to follow the example of his/her own belief, *or* a believer can be do so but also demand and consider him/herself as having, at least under certain conditions, the right to impose a belief upon others, with or without violence.

From these two different attitudes follow a range of very different options of behavior. It is reasonable to believe that the profound implications that follow from either position are likely to affect how a religion (or ideology) will act before a given problem or situation.

A second dimension concerns the substantial aspect of religion, often called theology, or just teachings. We are here looking at the self-understanding of the religious actor. The critical question would be: is a religious actor formulating a *credo* with regard to its responsiveness to the surrounding society, that is, in a contextualizing way, or not? Or is a religious actor formulating a *credo* without responsiveness to the surrounding society? In short, these alternatives could be labelled *contextualism* or *fanaticism*. These concepts refer in this context to whether someone is open to the needs of the society in a given situation, or if someone is fixed to ultimate and internally defined values or religious principles as a guide for teaching, without reference to the needs of the society.

Four positions are possible as a result of these two dimensions. Obviously, one extreme is a religion based on contextualizing teachings and with exposition as a way of living, the other extreme is a religion based on a fanatic interpretation formulated with a conviction of the need to impose one's views upon others. In a rainbow of possible propositions and hypotheses, it may be possible to get one step further in linking religion and war, in this way.

There is, finally, a dimension still to be identified, in our reflection on conditions for identifying the role of religion in relation to war and to peace. Jürgen Habermas has formulated it in a succinct way and his concern is the dialogue about and between religions themselves.

WHERE DOES IT ALL BEGIN?

Jürgen Habermas argues, in a discussion about the fine line between religion and naturalism, that the liberal state is dependent on pre-liberal historic processes in order to become liberal. Thus, the liberal state is in the long run dependent on mentalities which it cannot produce by itself. It has to postulate that those mentalities, of both religious and secular nature, exist on the basis of a historic developments. Habermas talks about the relations between secular and religious citizens, who all will have to accept fundamental conditions of mutual respect, rationality, and civility in their social behavior if the liberal state shall survive. But his argument is equally relevant for interreligious, and intercultural relations. According to Habermas, theology is critical for the formation of religious attitudes, basically only theology can do the pre-liberal formation work. Only theology can induce in religious believers civility and acceptance of the cognitive rules that allow coexistence of religions and cultures, including a secular one. Philosophy cannot enter this learning process of religions, it has to rely on intrareligious reflection and rationality.[46]

If Habermas is correct, we will need to develop more of peaceful theologies in order to create the preconditions that make up a structure of values that—like accountability, norms, and institutions do for the democratic peace—would create a stable foundation for peaceful interreligious and intercultural relations.

BIBLIOGRAPHY

Appleby, R. Scott. *The Ambivalence of the Sacred: Religion, Violence, and Reconciliation.* Lanham, MD: Rowman & Littlefield, 2000.

Balendra, Natasha. "Defining Armed Conflict." *Cardozo Law Review* 29/6 (May 2008) 2462–2512.

Bartolomeusz, Tessa J. *In Defense of Dharma: Just-War Ideology in Buddhist Sri Lanka.* London: Routledge, 2002.

Beeman, William O. "Fighting the Good Fight: Fundamentalism and Religious Revival." In *Anthropology for the Real World*, edited by J. MacClancy. Chicago: University Chicago Press, 2001. Online: http://www.brown.edu/Departments/Anthropology/publications/FUNDMNTALISM.htm.

Bell, Daniel, A. *Beyond Liberal Democracy: Political Thinking for an East Asian Context.* Princeton: Princeton University Press, 2006.

Bellin, Eva. "Faith in Politics. New Trends in the Study of Religion and Politics." *World Politics* 60 (January 2008) 315–47.

Blasi, Anthony J. "Definition of Religion." In *Encyclopedia of Religion and Society*, edited by Willam H. Swatos Jr., 129–32. Lanham, MD: Rowman & Littlefield, 1998.

Bush, George W. *Speech to a Joint Session of Congress, Sept. 20, 2001.* Online: http://middleeast.about.com/od/usmideastpolicy/a/bush-war-on-terror-speech.htm.

Cavanaugh, William T. *The Myth of Religious Violence: Secular Ideology and the Roots of Modern Conflict.* Oxford: University Press, 2009.

Duffy Toft, Monica. "Getting Religion? The Puzzling Case of Islam and Civil War." *International Security* 31/4 (Spring 2007) 97–131.

46. Habermas, *Mellan Naturalism och Religion*, 7ff.

Fox, Jonathan. *Religion, Civilization, and Civil War: 1945 Through the New Millennium.* Lanham, MD: Lexington, 2004.

Fox, Jonathan, and Shmuel Sandler, eds. *Bringing Religion Into International Relations.* New York: Palgrave MacMillan, 2004.

————, eds. *Religion in World Conflict.* London: Routledge, 2006.

Fukuyama, Francis. *The End of History and the Last Man.* New York: Avon, 1992.

Habermas, Jürgen. *Mellan Naturalism och Religion. Filosofiska uppsatser.* Uddevalla, Sweden: Daidalos, 2007.

Hanson, Eric O. *Religion and Politics in the International System Today.* Cambridge: Cambridge University Press, 2006.

Heinze, Eric A. "The Evolution of International Law in Light of the 'Global War on Terror.'" *Review of International Studies* 37/3 (July 2011) 1069–1094.

Huntington, Samuel P. "If Not Civilizations What? Samuel Huntington Responds to His Critics." *Foreign Affairs* 72/5 (Nov-Dec 1993) 186–94.

Juergensmeyer, Mark. *Terror in the Mind of God: The Global Rise of Religious Violence.* Berkeley: University of California Press, 2003.

King, Winston L. "Religion." In *Encyclopedia of Religion*, edited by Mircea Eliade, 12:284-85. New York: MacMillan, 1987.

Lektzian, David, and Mark Souva. "A Comparative Theory Test of Democratic Peace Arguments, 1946–2000." *Journal of Peace Research* 46/1 (January 2009) 17–37.

Marty, Martin E., and R. Scott Appleby, eds. *Fundamentalisms Comprehended.* Chicago: The University of Chicago Press, 2004.

Nordquist, Kjell-Åke. *Contradicting Peace Proposals in the Palestine Conflict.* Uppsala: Department of Peace and Conflict Research, 1985.

————. *From Just War to Justified Intervention: A Theory of International Responsibility.* Uppsala: Department of Theology, Uppsala University, 2005.

————. "Religion and Armed Conflict—Some Observations." In *States in Armed Conflict 1989*, edited by Karin Lindgren, 43–53. Report No. 32. Uppsala: Department of Peace and Conflict Research, 1991.

Norris, Pippa, and Ronald Inglehart. *Sacred and Secular: Religion and Politics Worldwide.* 2nd ed. Cambridge: Cambridge University Press, 2011.

Pettersson, Therése, and Lotta Themnér, eds. *States in Armed Conflict 2010.* Annual report, Uppsala Conflict Data Program. Uppsala: Department of Peace and Conflict Research, 2010.

Powers, Gerard F. "Religion and Peacebuilding." In *Strategies for Peace: Transforming Conflict in a Violent World,* edited by Daniel Philpott and Gerard F. Powers, 317–52. New York: Oxford University Press, 2010.

Ringgren, Helmer, and Åke V. Ström. *Religionerna i historia och nutid.* Arlöv, Sweden: Gothia, 1974.

Russett, Bruce, John R. Oneal, and Michaelene Cox. "Clash of Civilizations, or Realism and Liberalism Dejá-Vu? Some Evidence." *Journal of Peace Research* 37/5 (2000) 583–608.

Svensson, Isak. "Fighting with Faith: Religion and Conflict Resolution in Civil Wars." *Journal of Conflict Resolution* 51/6 (2007) 930–49.

Themnér, Lotta, and Peter Wallensteen. "Armed Conflict, 1946–2010." *Journal of Peace Research* 48/4 (2011) 525–36.

Vasquez, John A. "The Steps to War: Toward a Scientific Explanation of Correlates of War Findings." *World Politics* 40 (1987) 108–45.

Lightning Source UK Ltd.
Milton Keynes UK
UKOW06f1404150614

233450UK00005B/120/P